THE
Sixty Second
GRANDPARENT

Also by Rob Parsons

Bringing Home the Prodigals
Getting Your Kids Through Church Without Them Ending Up Hating God
Loving Against the Odds
Teenagers! What Every Parent *Has* to Know
The Heart of Success
The Money Secret
The Really *Really* Busy Person's Book on Marriage (with Katharine Hill)
The Really *Really* Busy Person's Book on Parenting (with Katharine Hill)
The Sixty Minute Debtbuster (with Katie Clarke)
The Sixty Minute Family
The Sixty Minute Father
The Sixty Minute Grandparent

The Sixty Minute Marriage
The Sixty Minute Mother
The Sixty Second Family
The Sixty Second Father
The Sixty Second Marriage
The Wisdom House
What Every Kid Wished Their Parents Knew ... and Vice Versa
What They Didn't Teach Me in Sunday School

And by Dianne Parsons
The Sixty Second Mother

THE *Sixty Second* GRANDPARENT

ROB PARSONS

Copyright © 2017 Rob Parsons

This edition published in 2019 by Care for the Family, Tovey House, Cleppa Park, Newport, NP10 8BA, UK. Web address: www.careforthefamily.org.uk.

The right of Rob Parsons to be identified as the author of the work has been asserted by him in accordance with the Copyright, Designs and Patents Act 1988.

All rights reserved. No part of this publication may be reproduced or transmitted in any form or by any means, electronic or mechanical, including photocopying, recording, or any information storage and retrieval system, without permission in writing from Care for the Family.

CONDITIONS OF SALE
This book is sold subject to the condition that it shall not, by way of trade or otherwise, be lent, re-sold, hired out or otherwise circulated without the publisher's prior consent in any form of binding or cover other than that in which it is published and without a similar condition including this condition being imposed on the subsequent purchaser.

ISBN 978-0-9932805-6-6
B1094

To David and Liliana and Nigel and Gay –
brilliant grandparents!

Acknowledgements

Special thanks to Alice Instone-Brewer and Sheron Rice for their fantastic help with this little collection of quotes. And many thanks also to designer Allison Hodgkiss, and Kim Davies, June Way and the team at Care for the Family.

"Grandparents are there to help the child get into mischief they haven't thought of yet." – Gene Perret

I love that quote – and I love being a grandparent! I now have five grandkids and, of course, I've realised that as the adult in the relationship, embracing acts of mischief is something to be practised on only a limited basis (but do look out for the opportunity when it comes!).

Of course, whenever we love, we open ourselves to the possibility of pain, and inevitably there are moments of worry and sadness as a grandparent. But there are also plenty of good times in which we experience the sheer joy, warmth and love that comes from having children in our lives.

This collection includes quotes from all sorts of people, some famous and others just like you and me. Whether or not you are a grandparent yourself, I do hope you enjoy it.

Rob Parsons, OBE

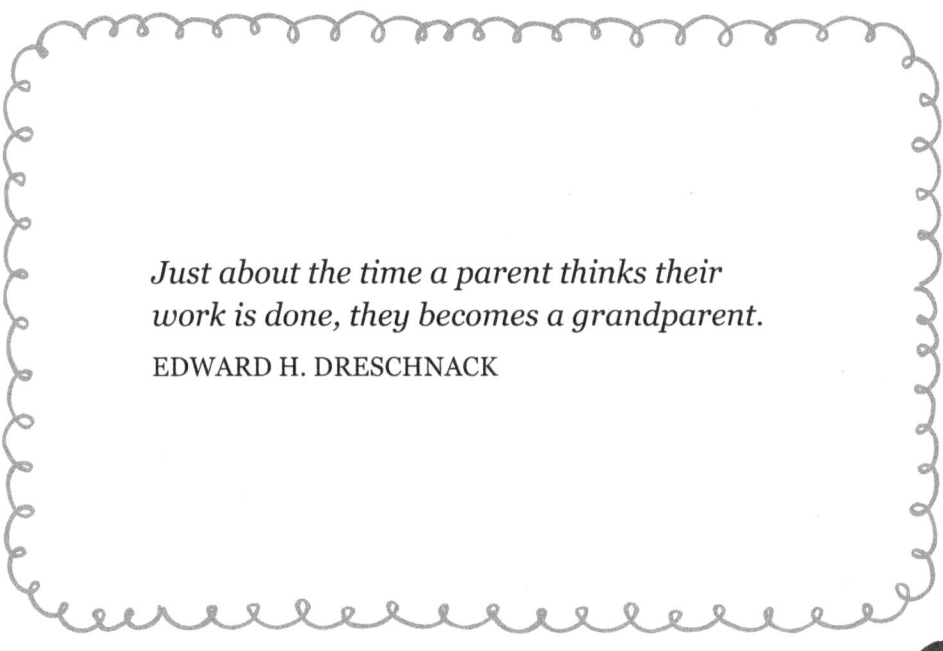

Just about the time a parent thinks their work is done, they becomes a grandparent.

EDWARD H. DRESCHNACK

There are all kinds of grandparents. Yes, there's still the grandma who interrupts her baking, wipes the flour from her hands onto her pinafore and gathers them to her bosom for a story. But there are also grandmothers who play in rock bands, run multinational corporations and sky-dive.

THE SIXTY SECOND GRANDPARENT

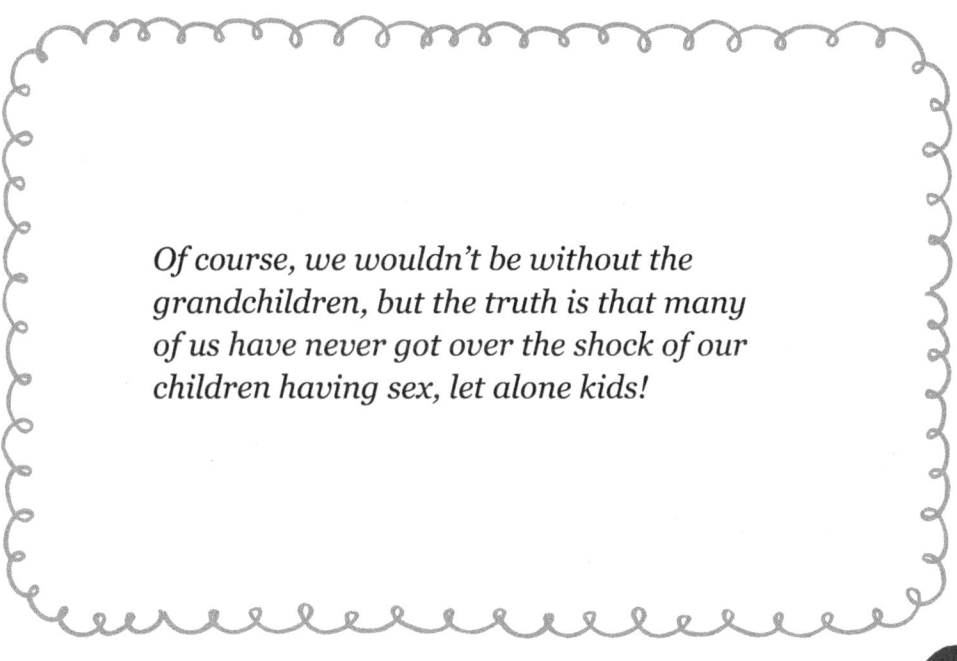

Of course, we wouldn't be without the grandchildren, but the truth is that many of us have never got over the shock of our children having sex, let alone kids!

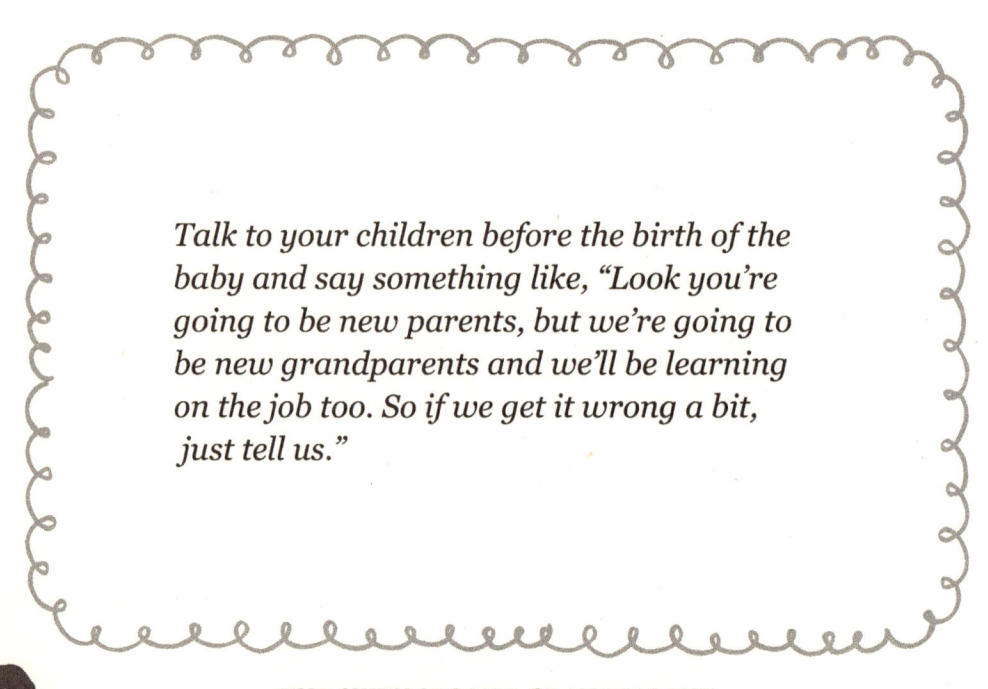

Talk to your children before the birth of the baby and say something like, "Look you're going to be new parents, but we're going to be new grandparents and we'll be learning on the job too. So if we get it wrong a bit, just tell us."

No cowboy was ever faster on the draw than a grandparent pulling a baby picture out of a wallet.

AUTHOR UNKNOWN

With so many people involved, it's as well to remember that the birth of a grandchild is not a competition for best gifts, most visits, or who the child most looks like. So when you see the child for the first time, try to resist the temptation to bag this new baby for your side of the family with comments like, "Oh, look at

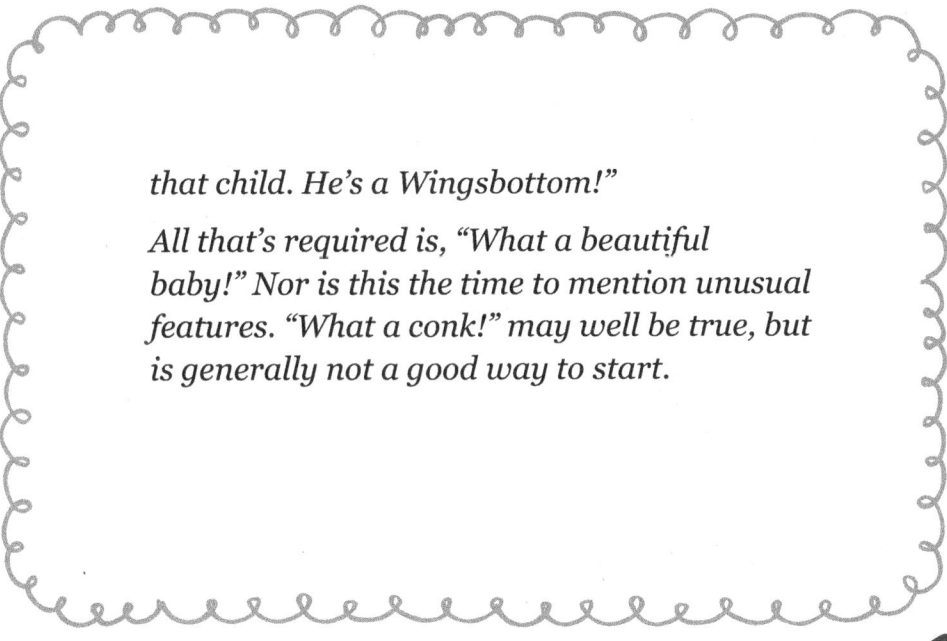

that child. He's a Wingsbottom!"

All that's required is, "What a beautiful baby!" Nor is this the time to mention unusual features. "What a conk!" may well be true, but is generally not a good way to start.

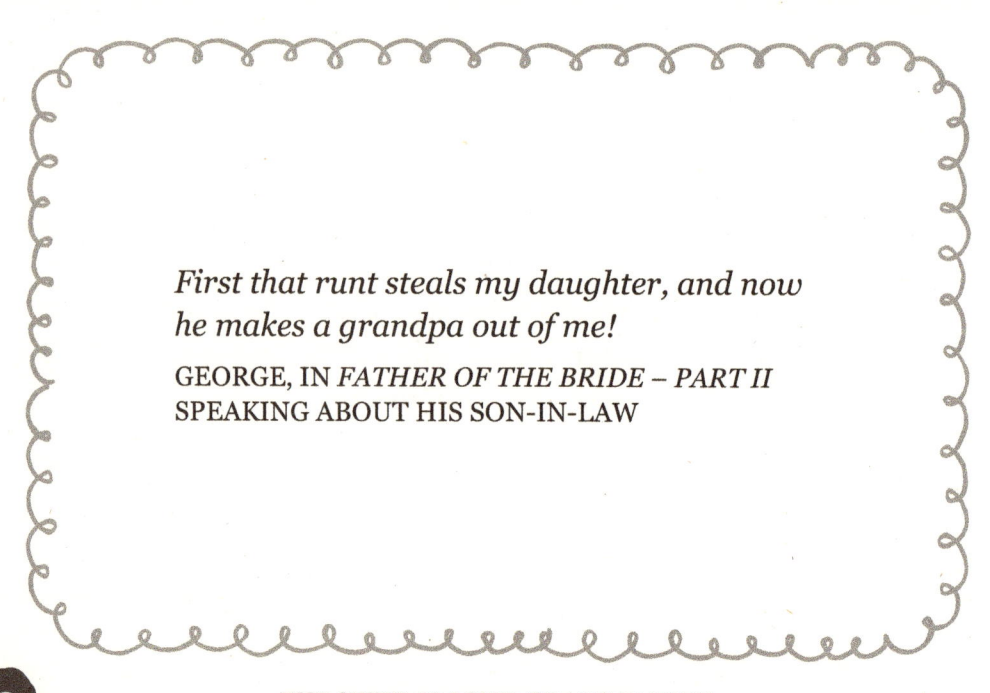

First that runt steals my daughter, and now he makes a grandpa out of me!

GEORGE, IN *FATHER OF THE BRIDE – PART II* SPEAKING ABOUT HIS SON-IN-LAW

It's worth remembering that your children may not be joking when they tell you the name they have chosen. Better to say, "Rooney? Perfect!" and risk looking naive, than to have to dig yourself out of a hole when you belatedly realise they are serious.

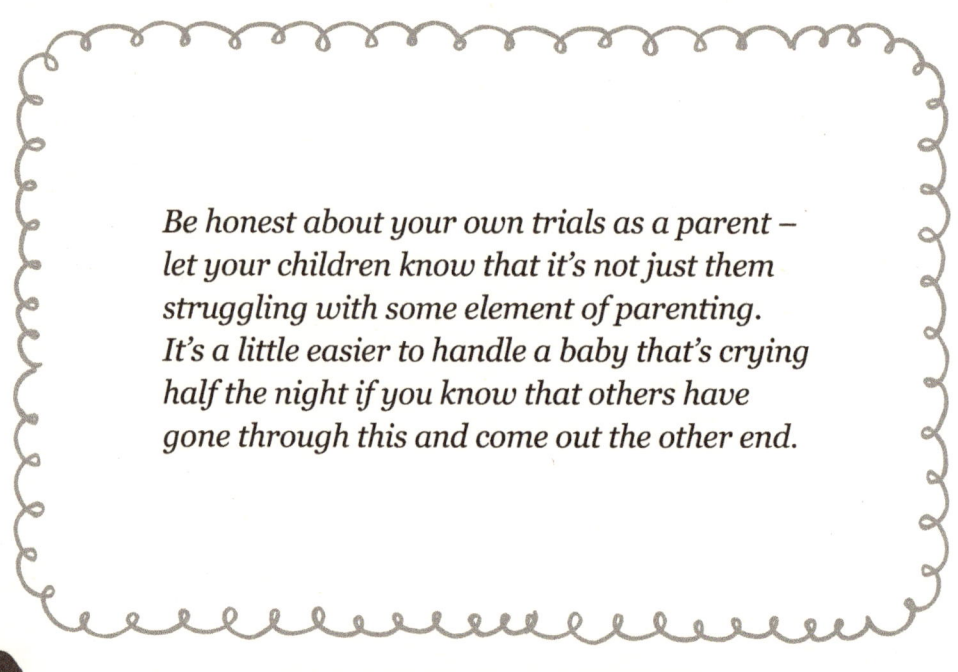

Be honest about your own trials as a parent – let your children know that it's not just them struggling with some element of parenting. It's a little easier to handle a baby that's crying half the night if you know that others have gone through this and come out the other end.

Where the pregnancy is a shock, even a sadness – at least at the time – what our children need then is not so much our joy as our unconditional love and support, and to know, above all, that we are with them in this.

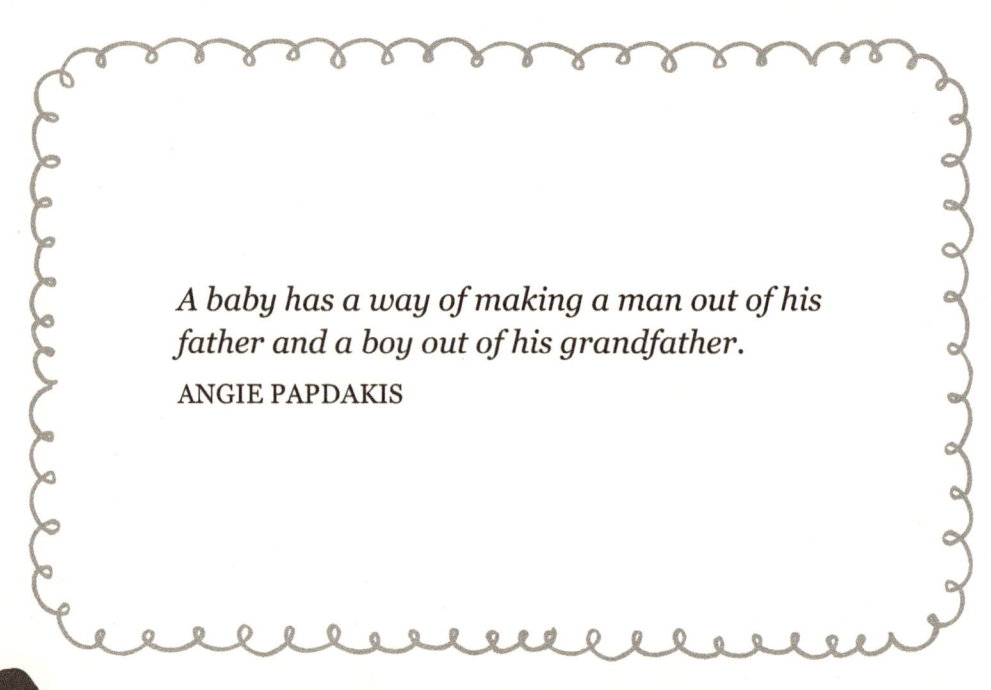

A baby has a way of making a man out of his father and a boy out of his grandfather.

ANGIE PAPDAKIS

There are grandparents who want to be involved as much as possible, and some who are scared to death that they might have to be. There are grandparents who feel confident about the tasks ahead, and those who are fearful they might make a dreadful mistake. But although different, each of us has the same aspiration: to be the best grandparent that we can be.

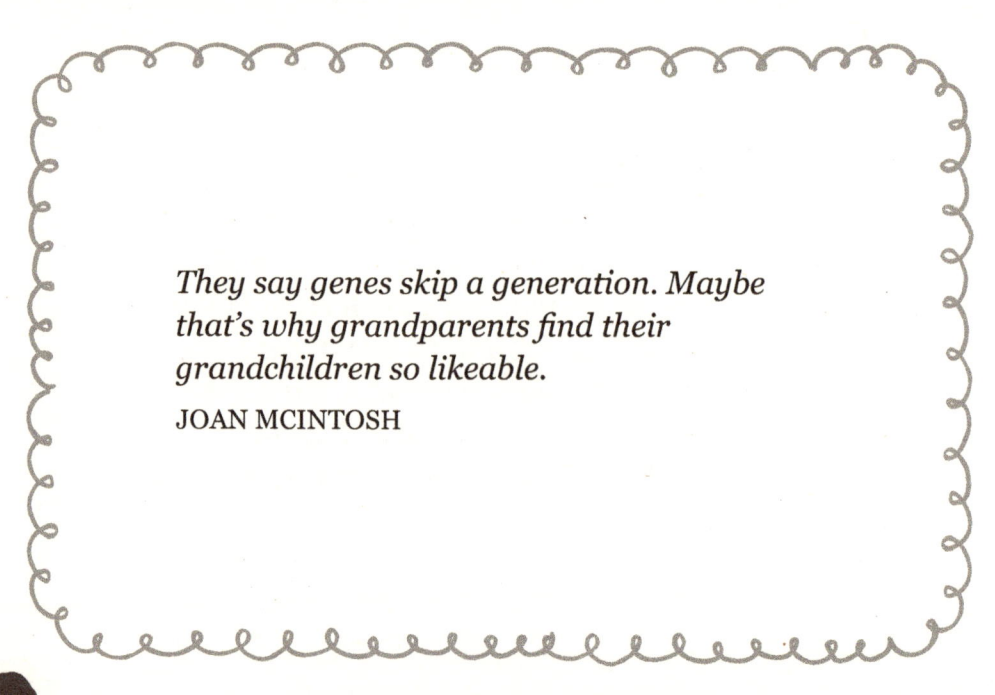

They say genes skip a generation. Maybe that's why grandparents find their grandchildren so likeable.

JOAN MCINTOSH

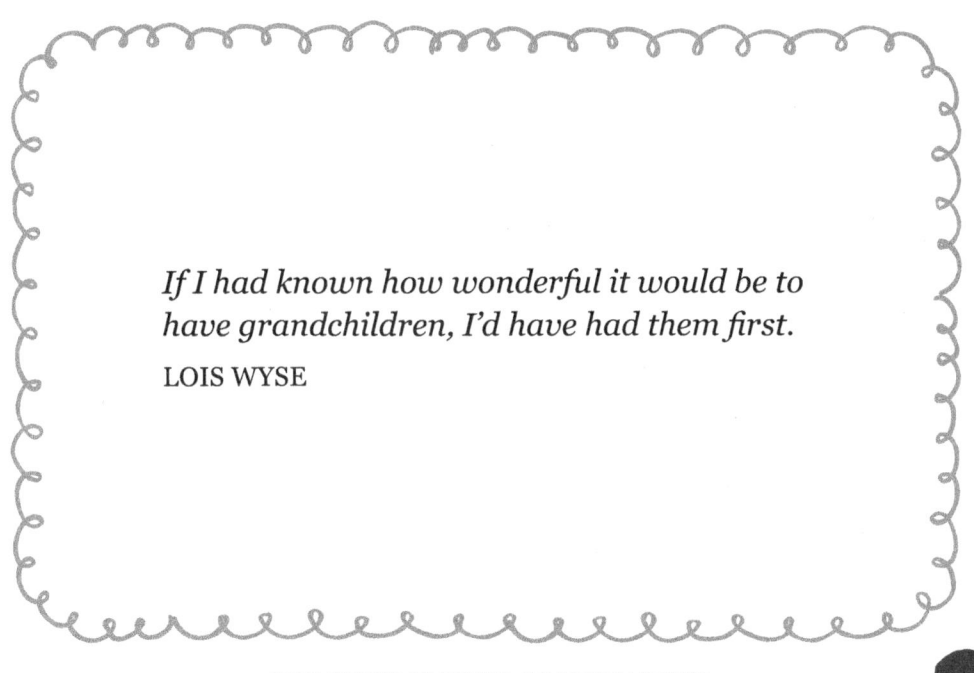

If I had known how wonderful it would be to have grandchildren, I'd have had them first.

LOIS WYSE

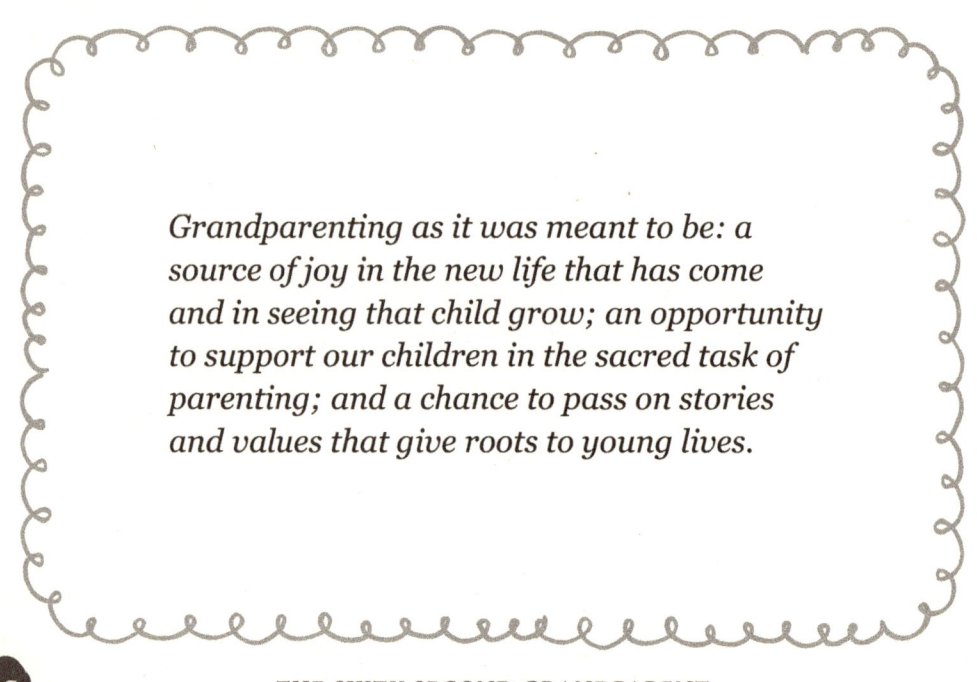

Grandparenting as it was meant to be: a source of joy in the new life that has come and in seeing that child grow; an opportunity to support our children in the sacred task of parenting; and a chance to pass on stories and values that give roots to young lives.

*Give a family with a new baby **space**.*

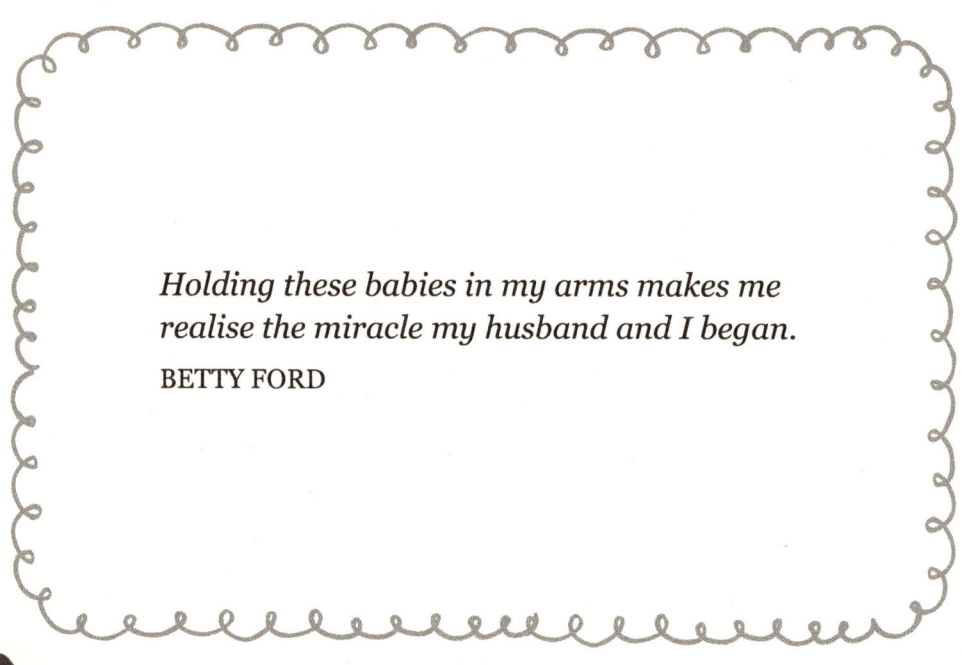

Holding these babies in my arms makes me realise the miracle my husband and I began.

BETTY FORD

Children will forgive you almost anything – from facial hair to picking them up from school in a three-wheeled Reliant Robin – so long as they believe in their hearts the two things that really matter to a child:

"My Gran and Granddad love me."

"Granny and Grandpa are always there for me."

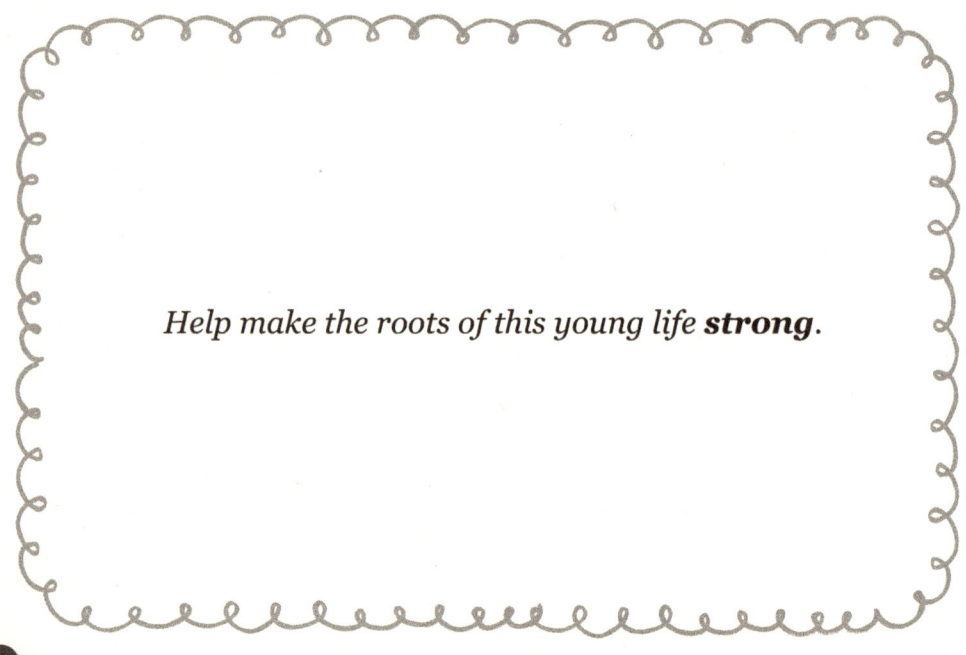

*Help make the roots of this young life **strong**.*

THE SIXTY SECOND GRANDPARENT

Let us make future generations remember us as proud ancestors just as, today, we remember our forefathers.

ROH MOO-HYUN

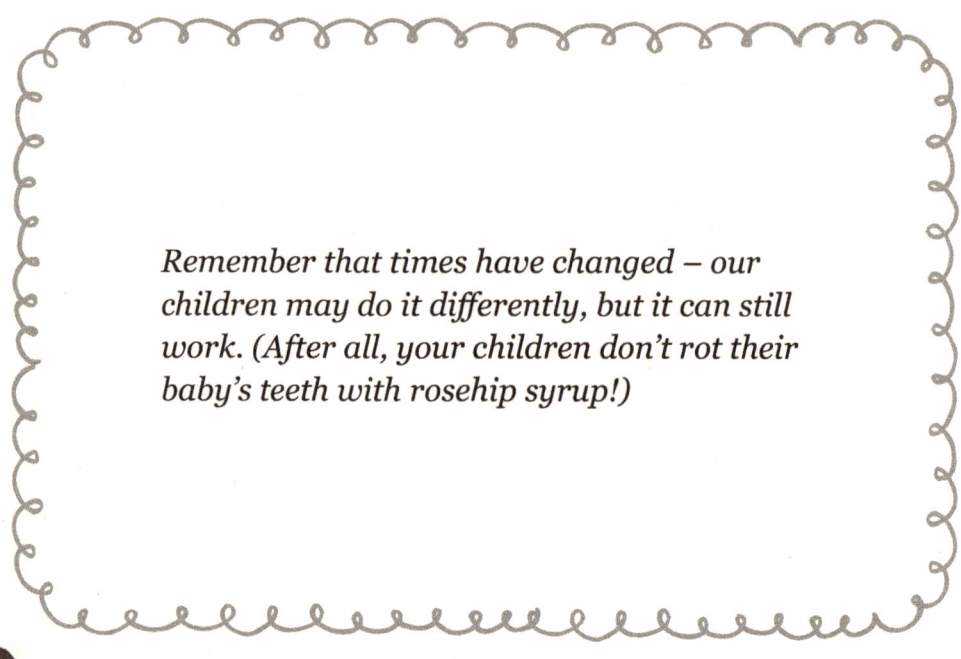

Remember that times have changed – our children may do it differently, but it can still work. (After all, your children don't rot their baby's teeth with rosehip syrup!)

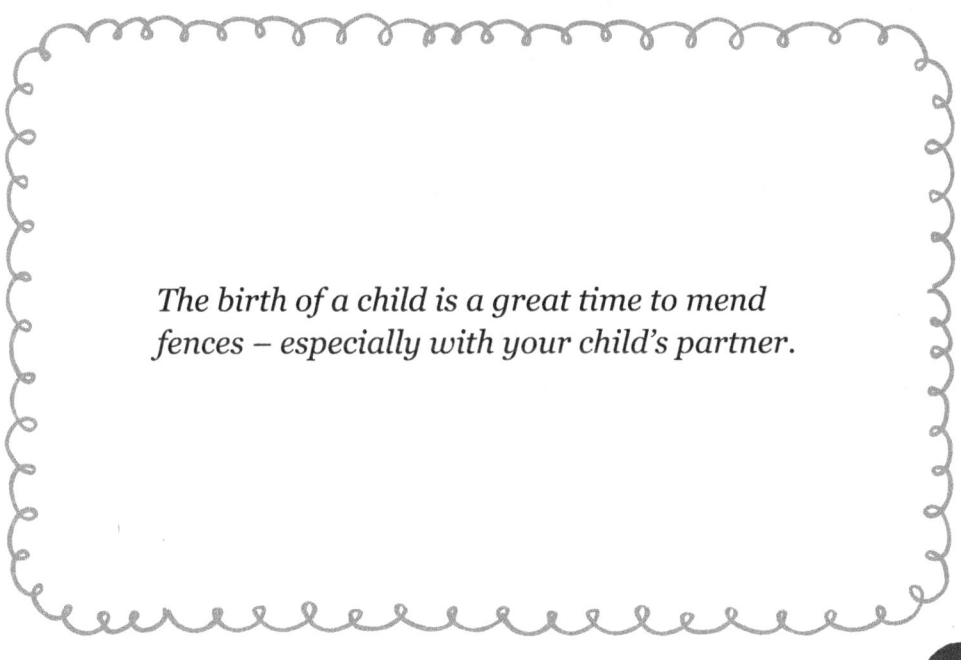

The birth of a child is a great time to mend fences – especially with your child's partner.

My granddaughter talked excitedly to her aunty Margaret about what my husband and I had given her for her birthday. Margaret was generally cross-tempered and disapproving, and she soon interrupted her. "You're spoilt!" she hissed.

*"Yes, I know," my granddaughter replied after a short pause. "Grandma and Grandpa do spoil me – **and I like it!**"*

AUTHOR UNKNOWN

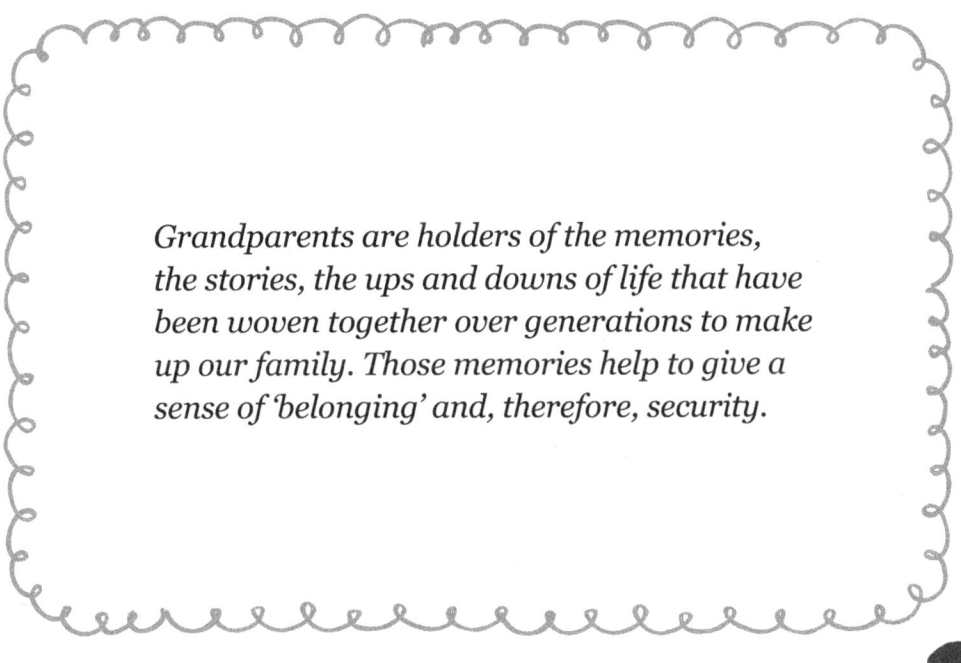

Grandparents are holders of the memories, the stories, the ups and downs of life that have been woven together over generations to make up our family. Those memories help to give a sense of 'belonging' and, therefore, security.

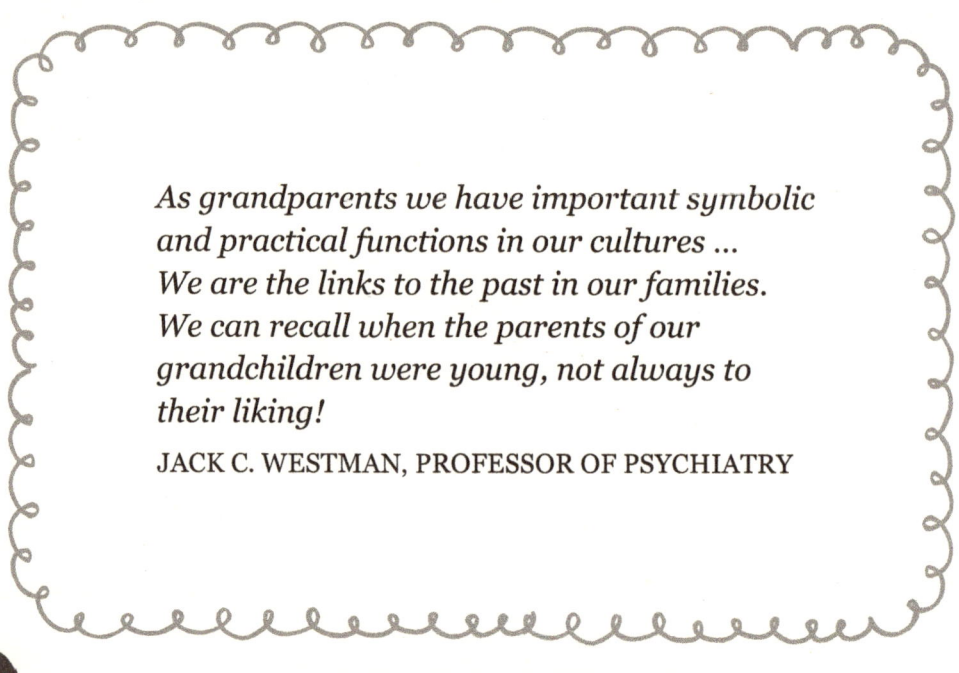

*As grandparents we have important symbolic and practical functions in our cultures ...
We are the links to the past in our families.
We can recall when the parents of our grandchildren were young, not always to their liking!*

JACK C. WESTMAN, PROFESSOR OF PSYCHIATRY

Grandparents don't have to be smart, only answer questions like why do dogs hate cats and how come God isn't married.

AUTHOR UNKNOWN

Even young grandparents seem enormously old to a small child, although the child may politely deny it. One small girl, feeling proud of reaching the monumental age of four, turned to her young-looking grandmother and asked, "How come I'm so old if you're so new?"

ALISON JUDSON RYERSON

In African culture there is a saying: "When an old person dies, it is as if a library burns down." But the library shouldn't burn down. One of the most valuable things a grandparent can do is to record the past for future generations – so make sure you record it.

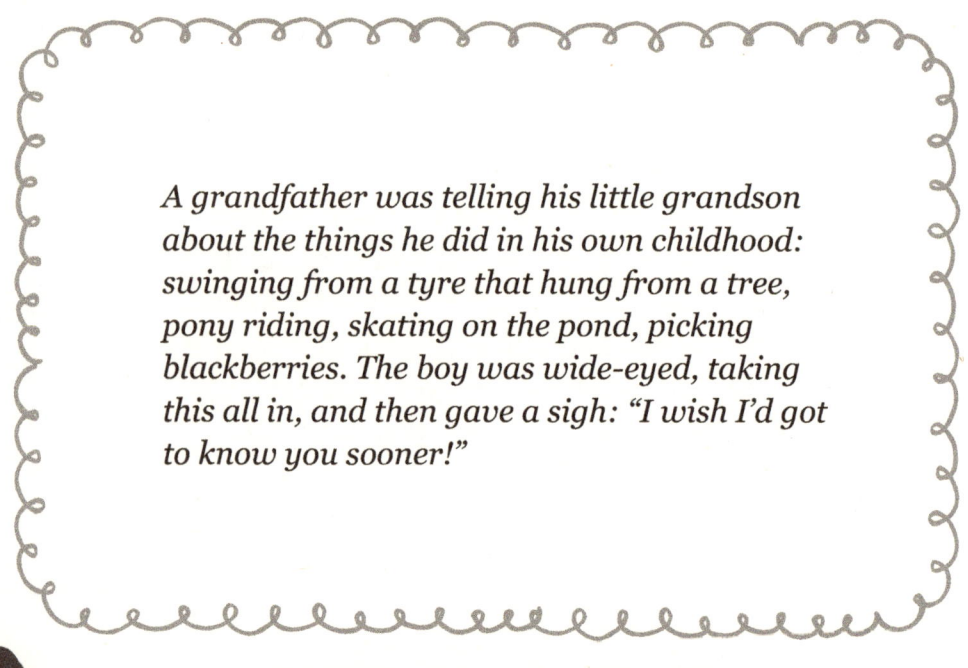

A grandfather was telling his little grandson about the things he did in his own childhood: swinging from a tyre that hung from a tree, pony riding, skating on the pond, picking blackberries. The boy was wide-eyed, taking this all in, and then gave a sigh: "I wish I'd got to know you sooner!"

THE SIXTY SECOND GRANDPARENT

I love this child. Red-haired, patient and gentle like her mother, fey and funny like her father. When she giggles I can hear him when he and I were young. I am part of this child. It may be only because we share genes and therefore smell familiar to each other ... It may be that a part of me lives in her in some important way ... But for now, it's jelly beans and 'Old MacDonald' that unite us.

ROBERT FULGHUM

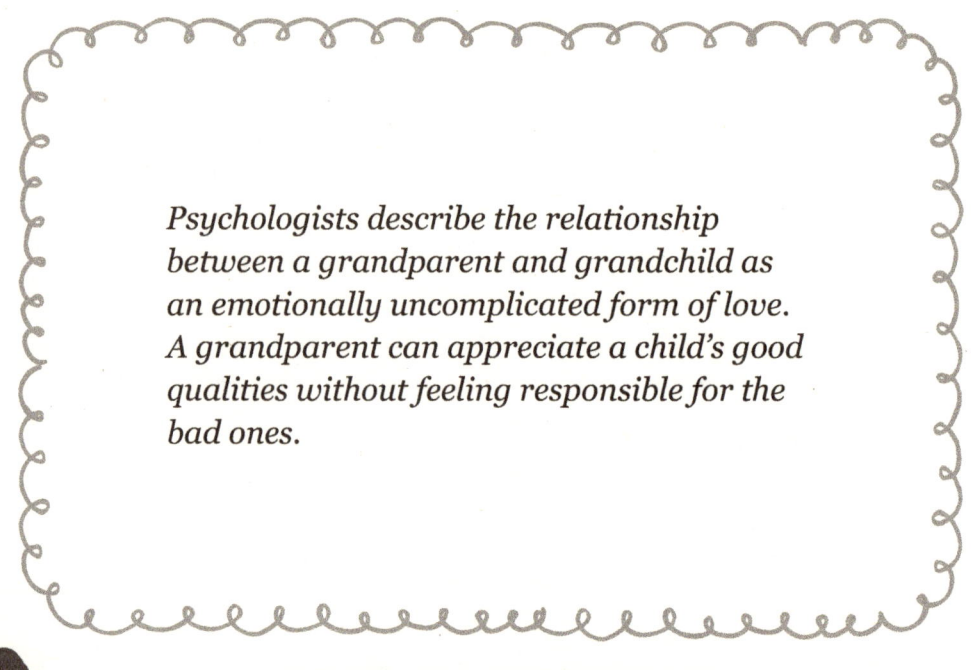

Psychologists describe the relationship between a grandparent and grandchild as an emotionally uncomplicated form of love. A grandparent can appreciate a child's good qualities without feeling responsible for the bad ones.

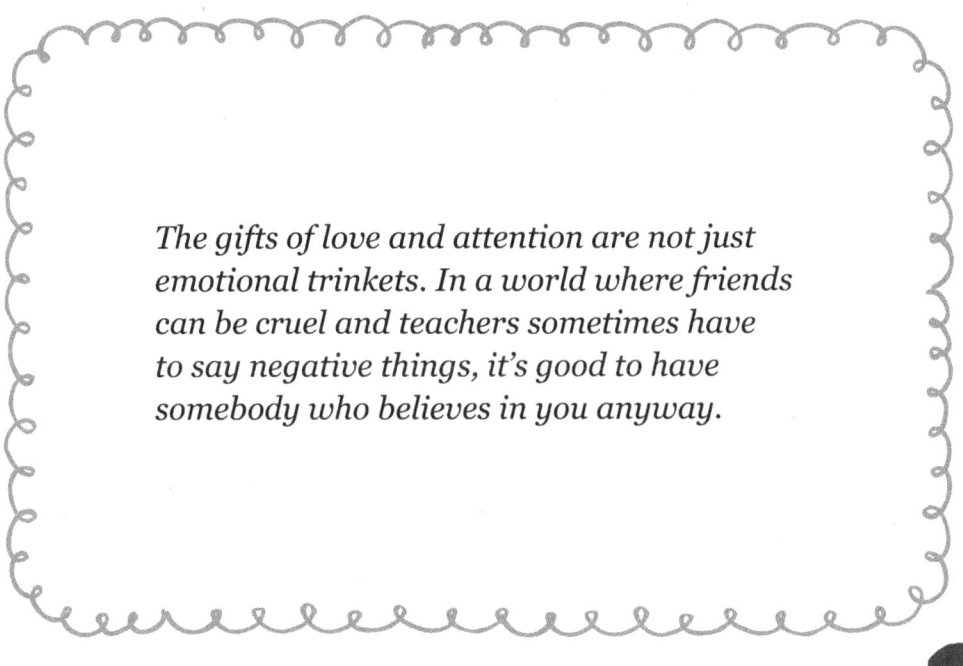

The gifts of love and attention are not just emotional trinkets. In a world where friends can be cruel and teachers sometimes have to say negative things, it's good to have somebody who believes in you anyway.

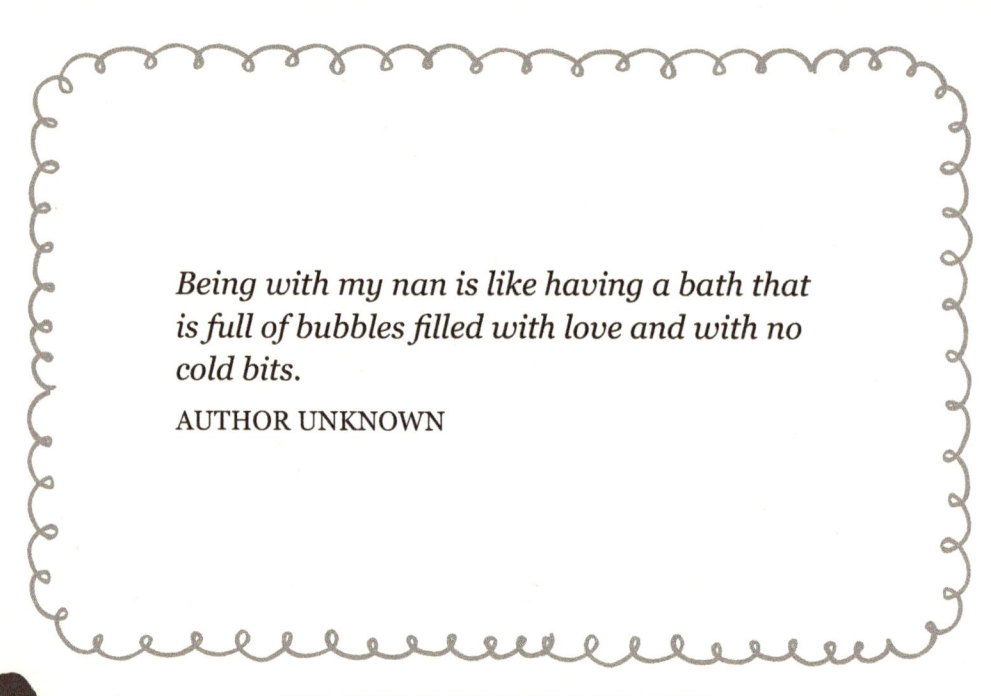

Being with my nan is like having a bath that is full of bubbles filled with love and with no cold bits.

AUTHOR UNKNOWN

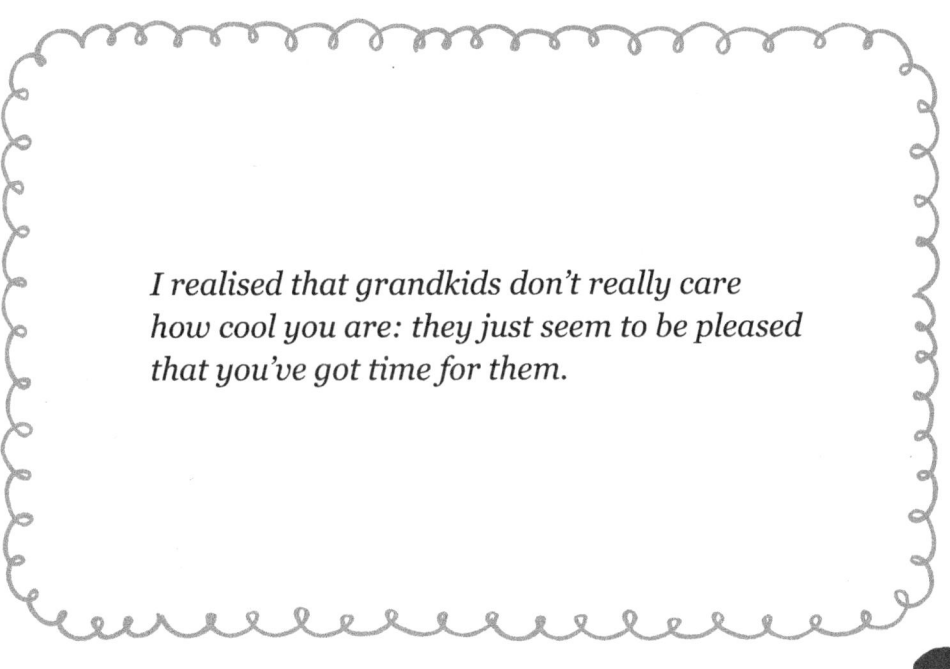

I realised that grandkids don't really care how cool you are: they just seem to be pleased that you've got time for them.

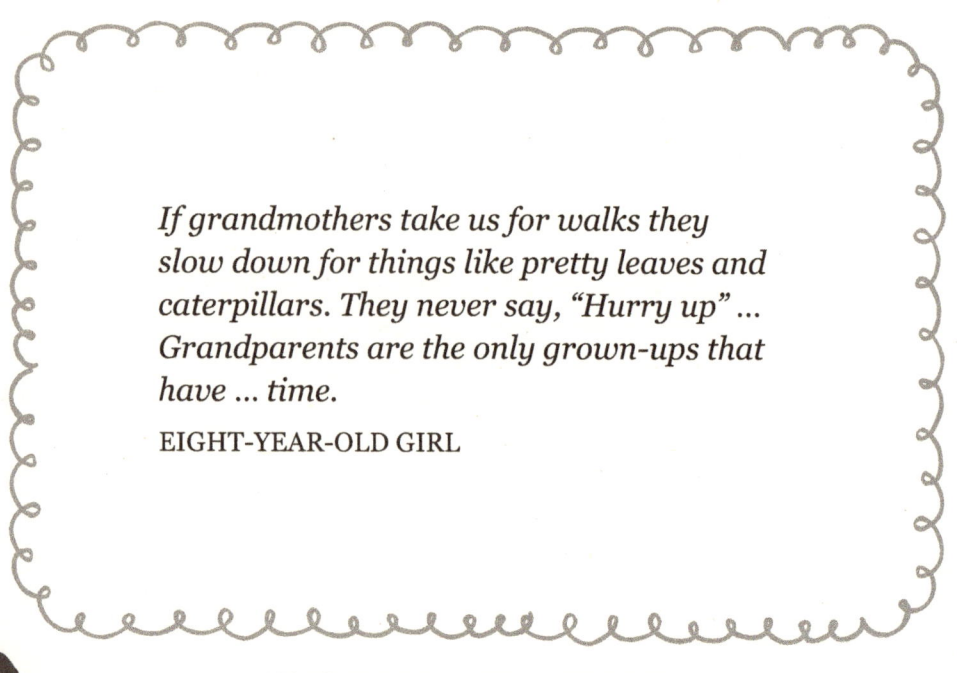

If grandmothers take us for walks they slow down for things like pretty leaves and caterpillars. They never say, "Hurry up" ... Grandparents are the only grown-ups that have ... time.

EIGHT-YEAR-OLD GIRL

Whether it's model-making, knitting, trainspotting or origami, the great thing about getting your grandchild involved in your hobby is that unlike watching The Lion King *fifty-four times, you **both** actually enjoy it.*

My granddaughter came to spend a few weeks with me, and I decided to teach her to sew. After I had gone through a lengthy explanation of how to thread the machine, she stepped back, put her hands on her hips, and said in disbelief, "You mean you can do all that, but you can't play my Game Boy?"

AUTHOR UNKNOWN

I have never once regretted missing a business opportunity so that I could be with my children and grandchildren.

MITT ROMNEY

Because [grandparents] are usually free to love and guide and befriend the young without having to take daily responsibility for them, they can often reach out past pride and fear of failure and close the space between generations.

JIMMY CARTER

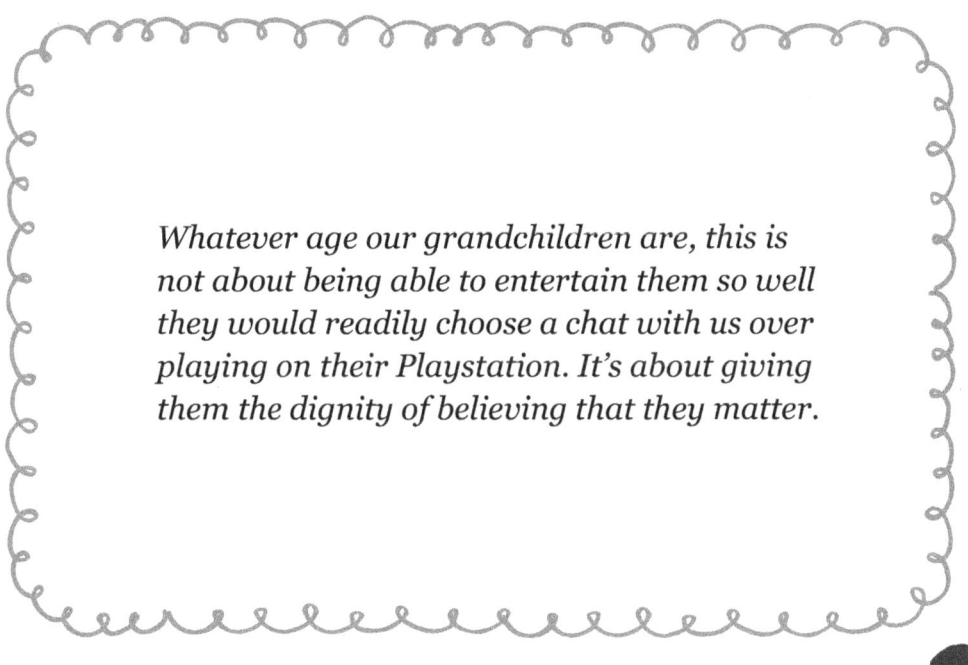

Whatever age our grandchildren are, this is not about being able to entertain them so well they would readily choose a chat with us over playing on their Playstation. It's about giving them the dignity of believing that they matter.

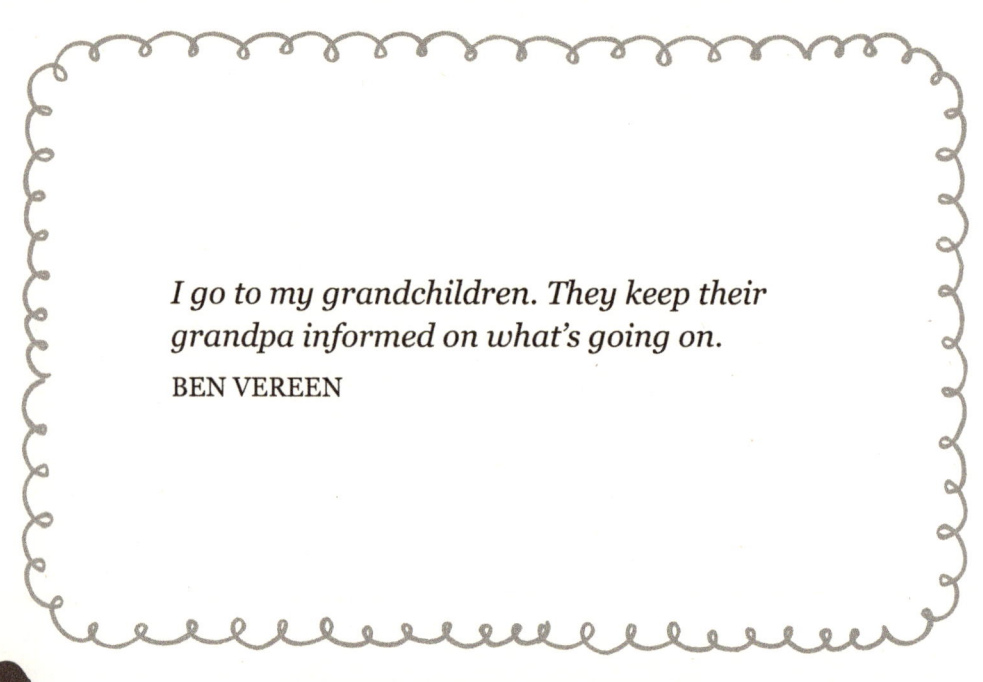

I go to my grandchildren. They keep their grandpa informed on what's going on.

BEN VEREEN

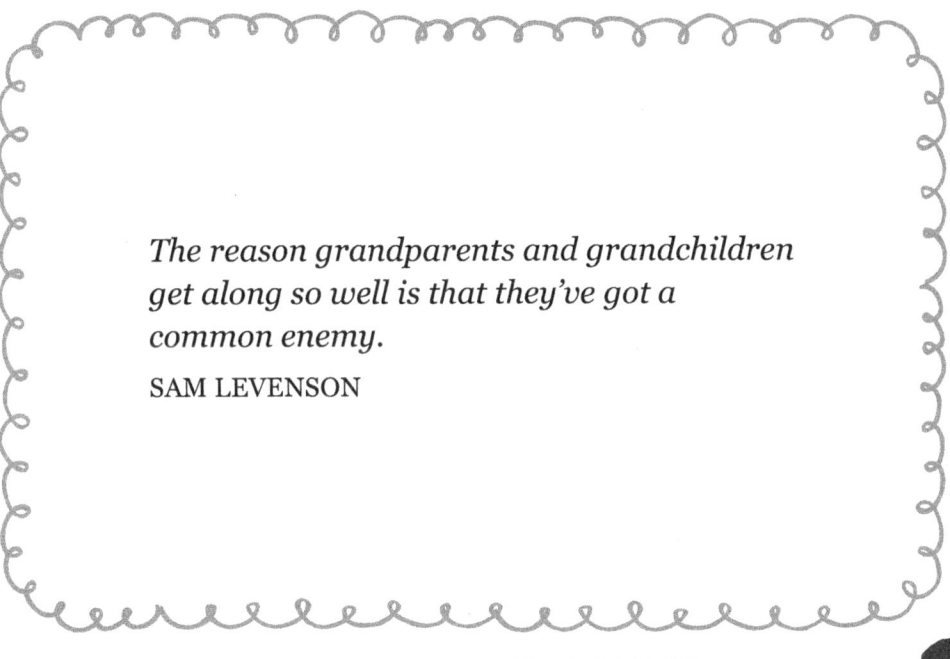

The reason grandparents and grandchildren get along so well is that they've got a common enemy.

SAM LEVENSON

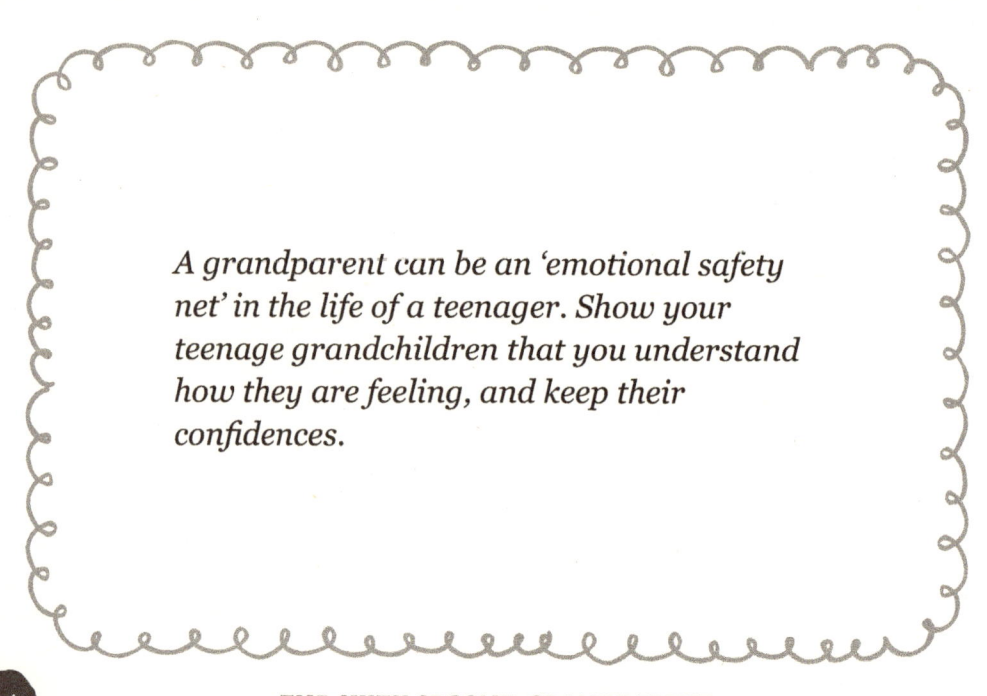

A grandparent can be an 'emotional safety net' in the life of a teenager. Show your teenage grandchildren that you understand how they are feeling, and keep their confidences.

THE SIXTY SECOND GRANDPARENT

Unconditional love is the most powerful force in the world. In a world that can bully us, measure us, assess us, judge us and demand one more trick when our bag of magic is already empty, a grandparent can be someone who loves us anyway.

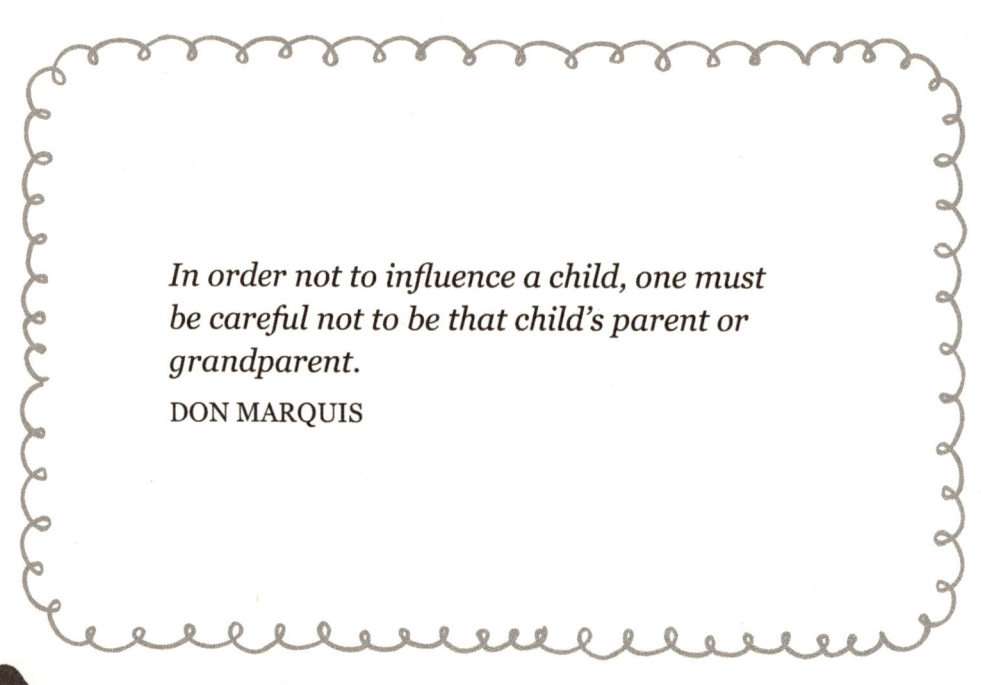

In order not to influence a child, one must be careful not to be that child's parent or grandparent.

DON MARQUIS

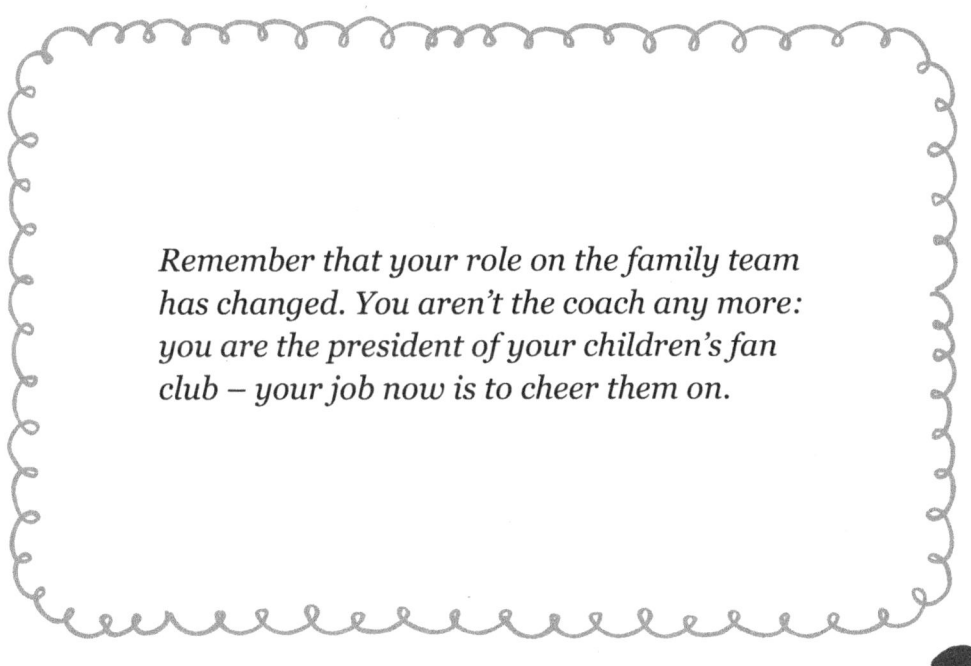

Remember that your role on the family team has changed. You aren't the coach any more: you are the president of your children's fan club – your job now is to cheer them on.

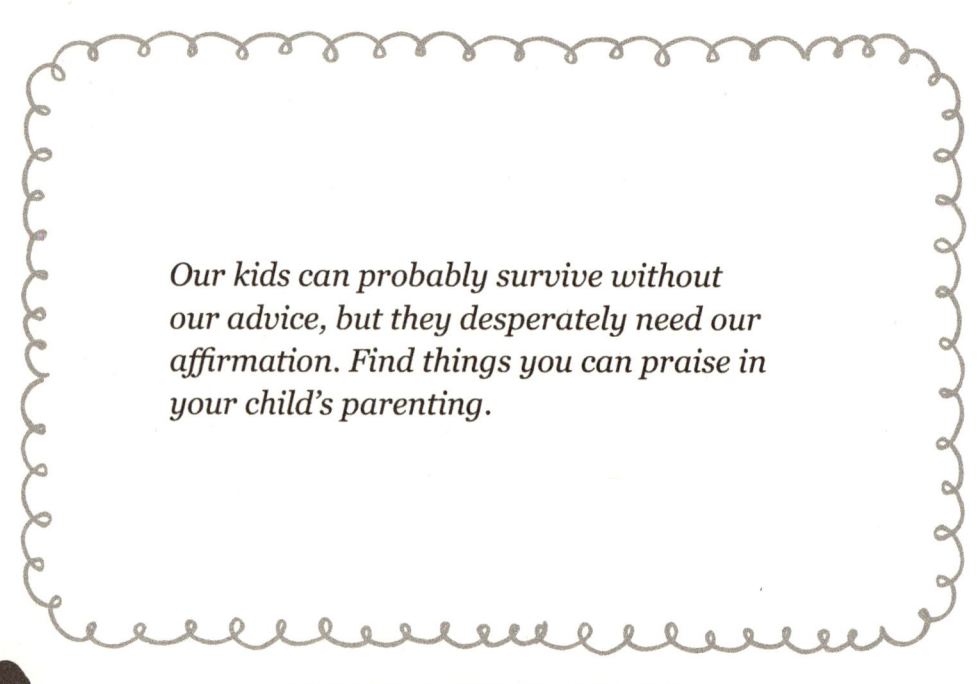

Our kids can probably survive without our advice, but they desperately need our affirmation. Find things you can praise in your child's parenting.

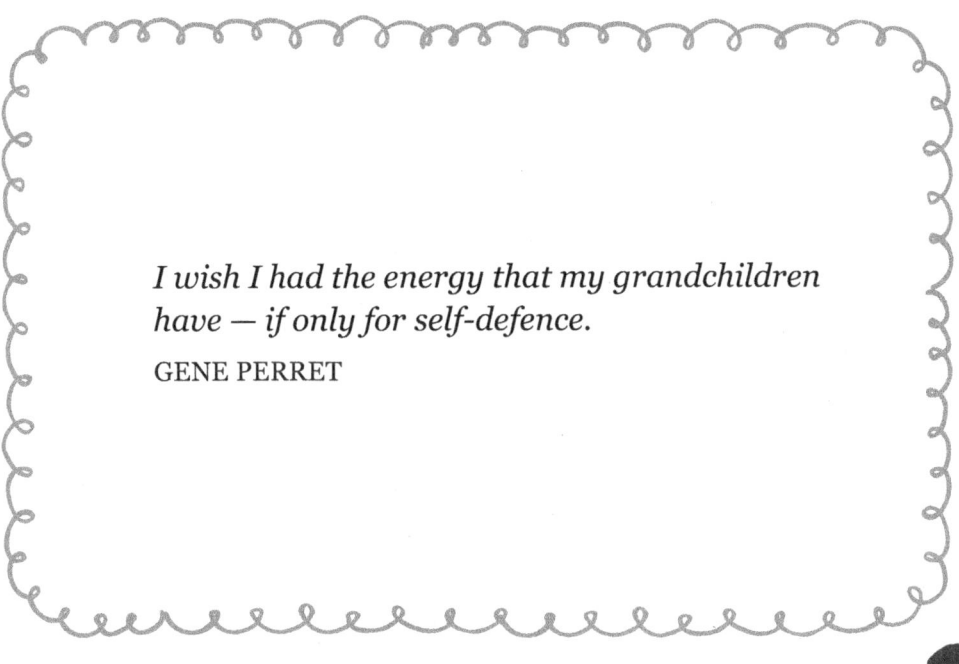

I wish I had the energy that my grandchildren have — if only for self-defence.

GENE PERRET

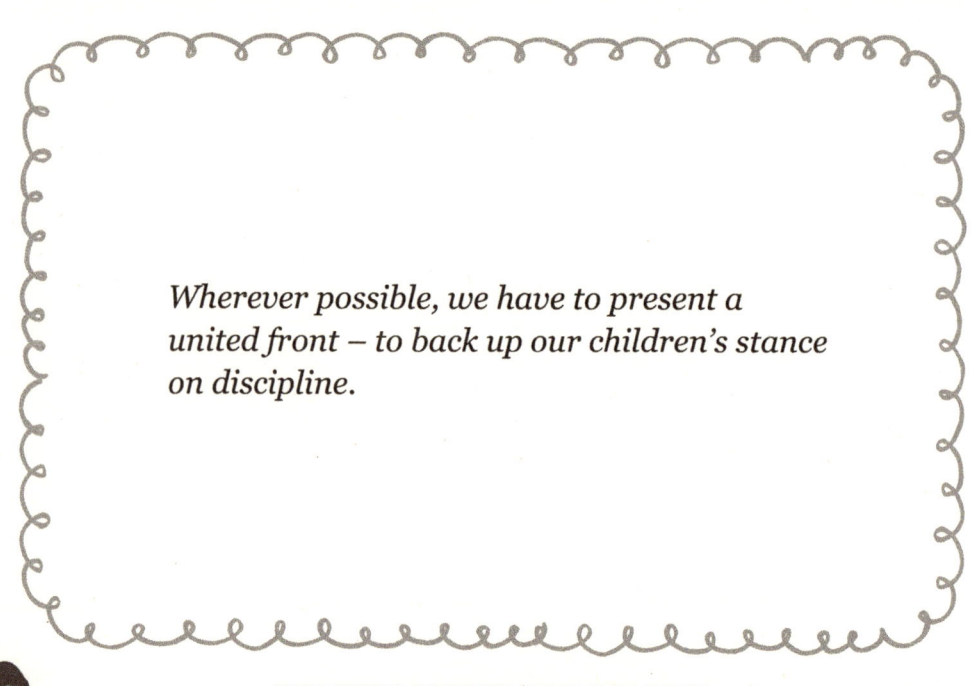

Wherever possible, we have to present a united front – to back up our children's stance on discipline.

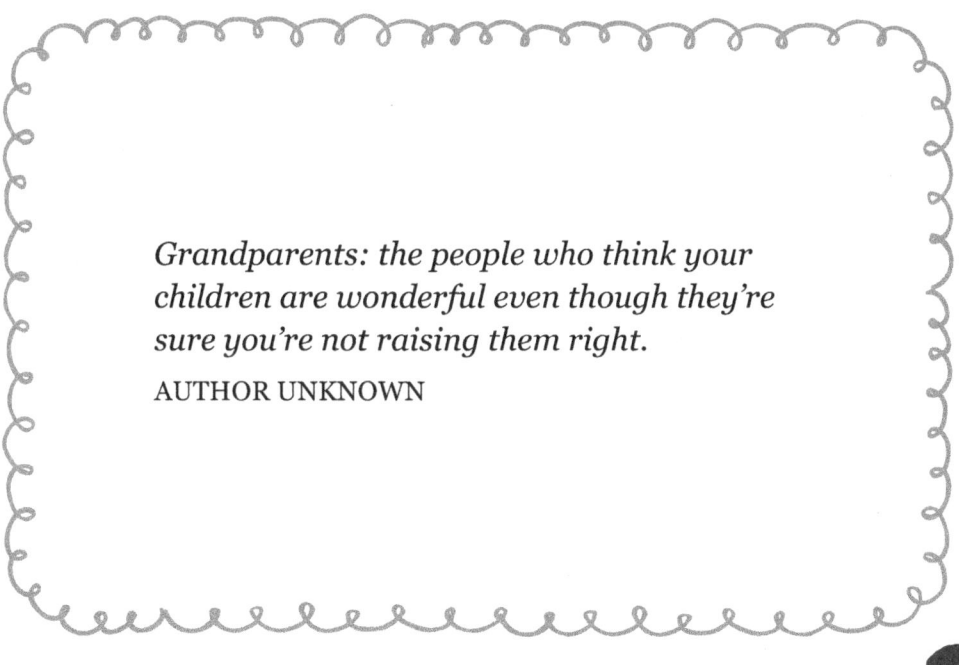

Grandparents: the people who think your children are wonderful even though they're sure you're not raising them right.

AUTHOR UNKNOWN

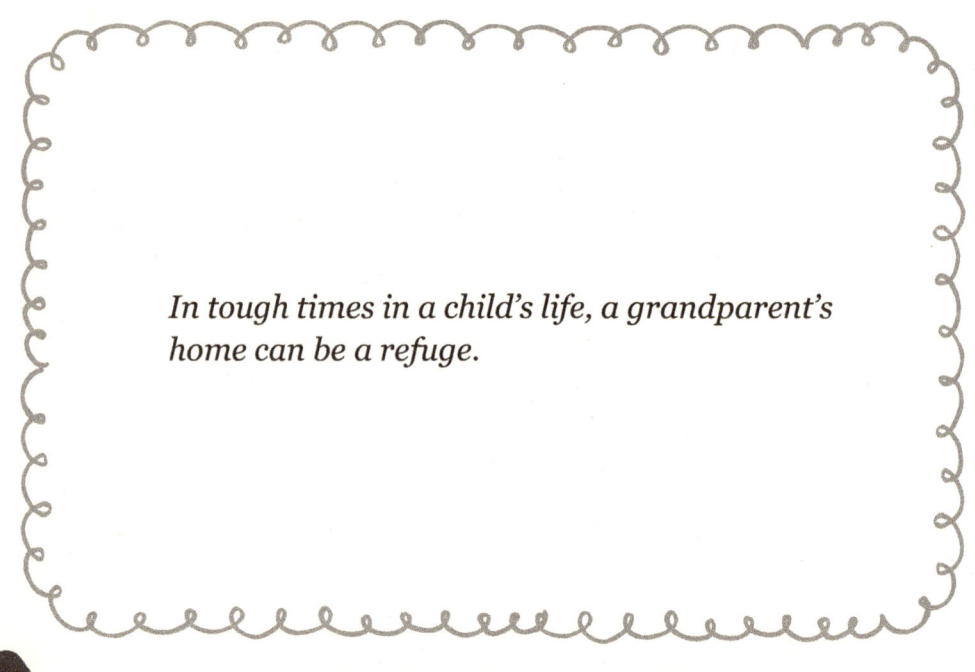

In tough times in a child's life, a grandparent's home can be a refuge.

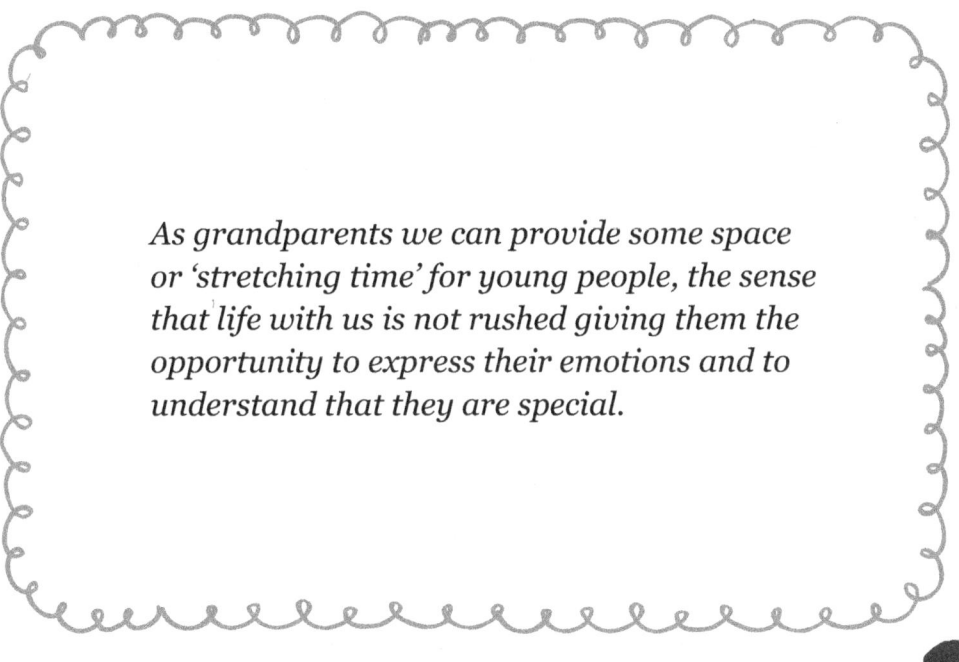

As grandparents we can provide some space or 'stretching time' for young people, the sense that life with us is not rushed giving them the opportunity to express their emotions and to understand that they are special.

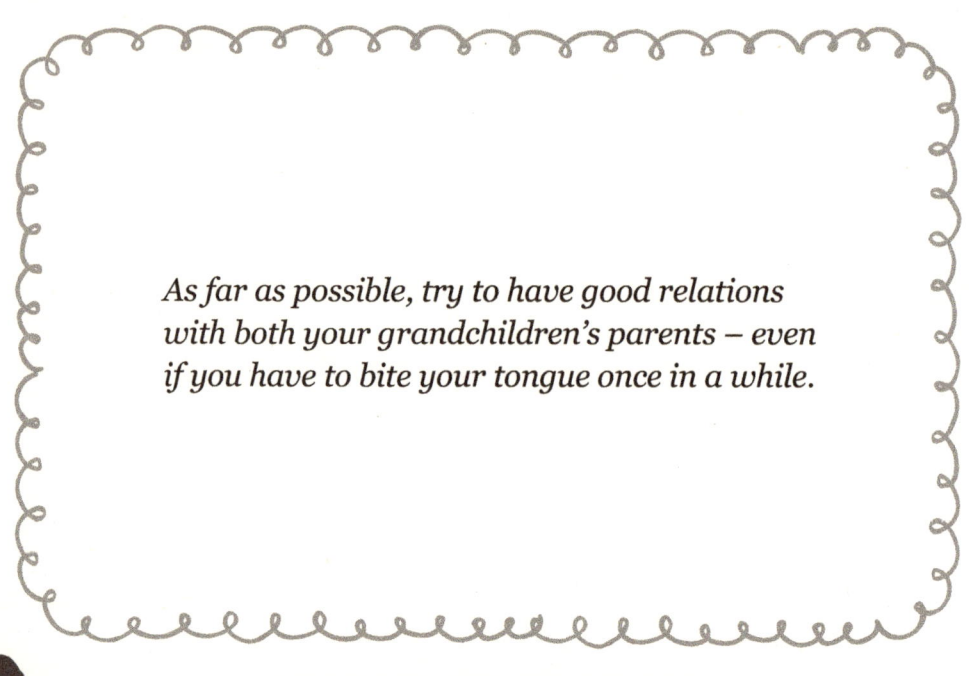

As far as possible, try to have good relations with both your grandchildren's parents – even if you have to bite your tongue once in a while.

Grandkids bring you into a sweeter, slower present. They show you the future at a time when a lot of your friends are thinking about the past. And they take you back to childhood – theirs, the parent's, your own: a three-time admittance to wonderland.

ADAIR LARA

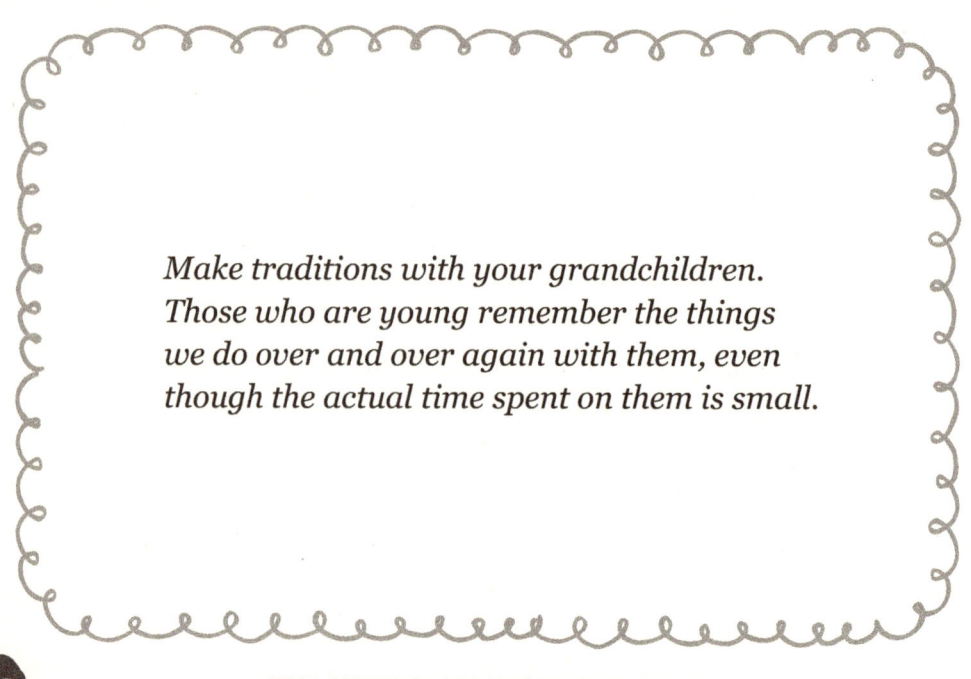

Make traditions with your grandchildren. Those who are young remember the things we do over and over again with them, even though the actual time spent on them is small.

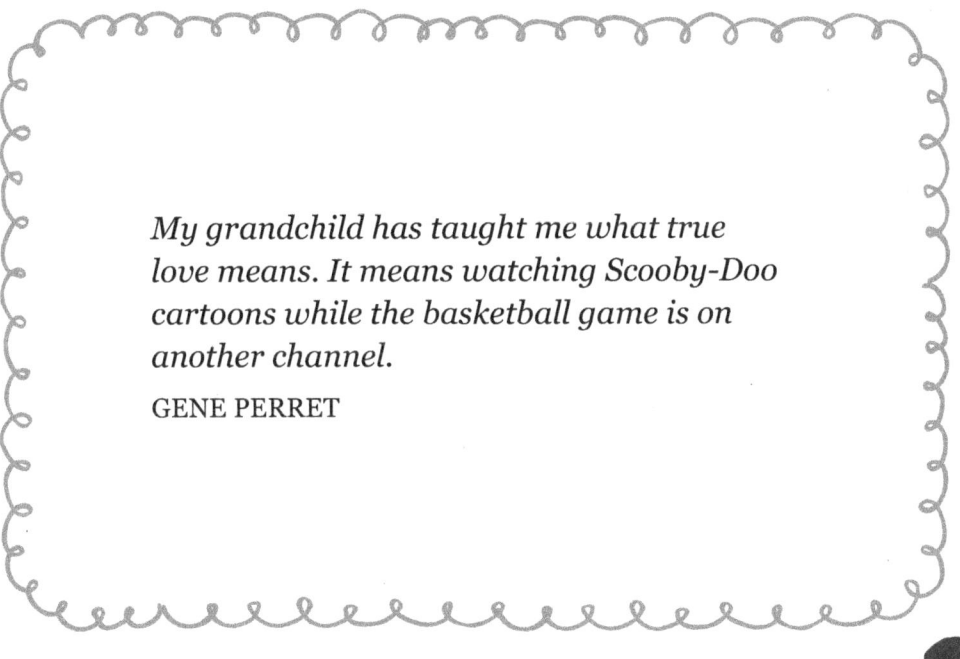

My grandchild has taught me what true love means. It means watching Scooby-Doo cartoons while the basketball game is on another channel.

GENE PERRET

A grandmother went to watch her grandson at the school sports day. Tom didn't get into the final of the 100 metres or the 200 metres, and he was unplaced in the longer races as well. In fact, the only event in which he looked remotely comfortable was the egg-and-spoon race, but even then he came last.

As Tom and his grandmother walked away together, the little boy's head was down until she put her arm around him and whispered, "You were the only one whose egg didn't fall off the spoon."

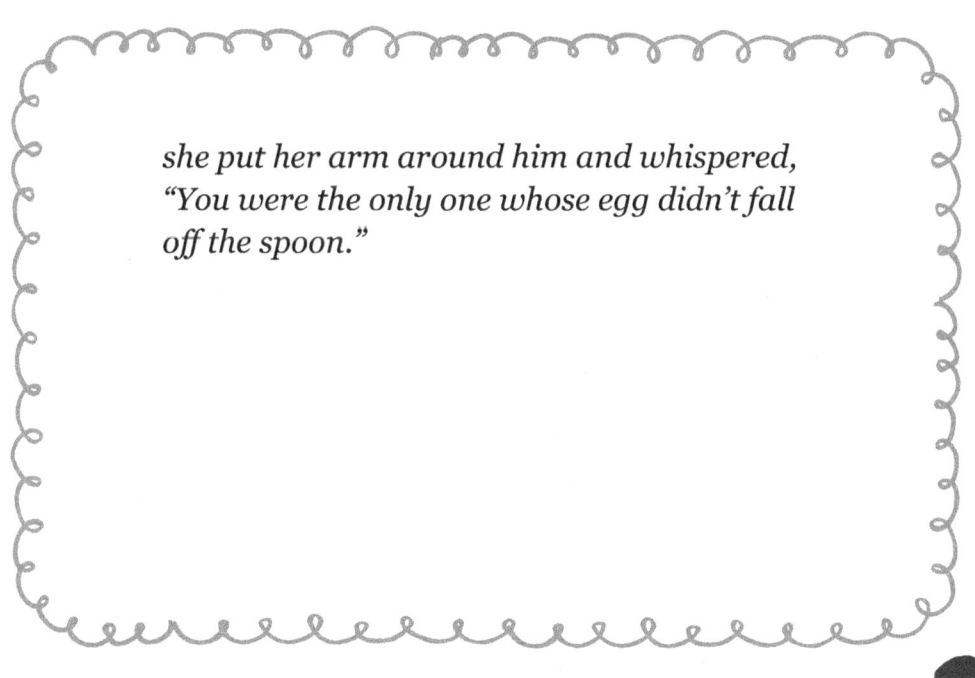

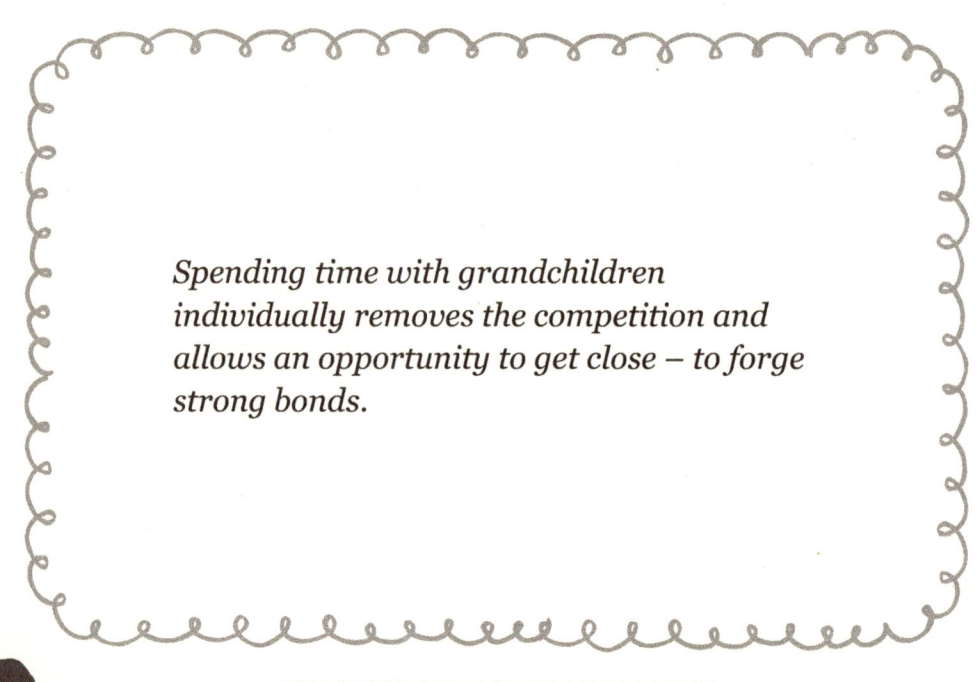

Spending time with grandchildren individually removes the competition and allows an opportunity to get close – to forge strong bonds.

Step-grandparents can have a wonderful healing role in families. If we are prepared at first simply to be a new friend to a child, we may well become not only part of the healing process, but also, while that process is happening, a refuge.

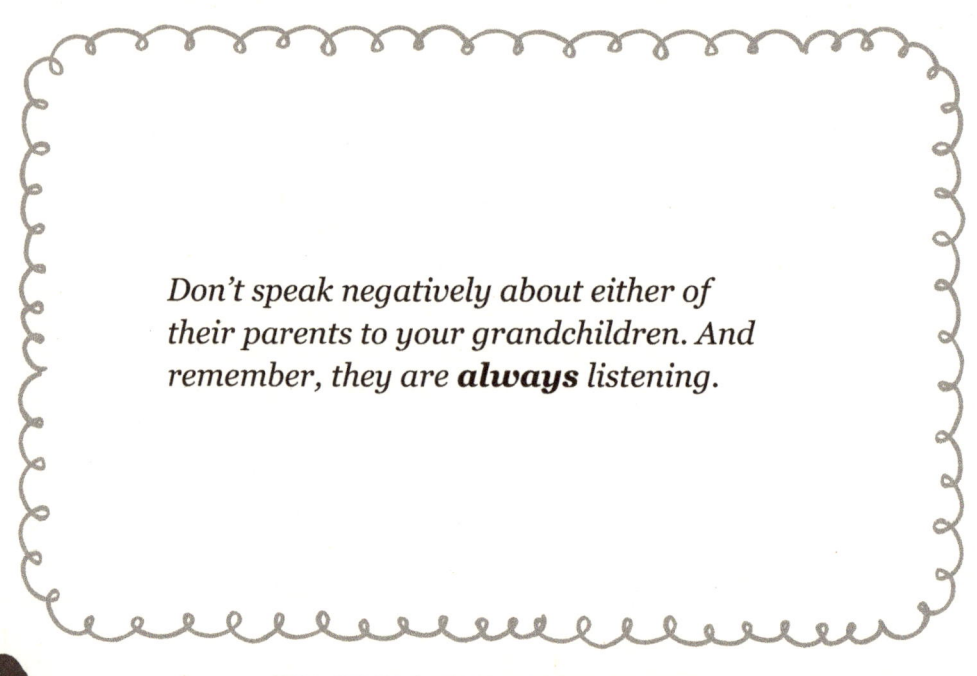

*Don't speak negatively about either of their parents to your grandchildren. And remember, they are **always** listening.*

My mother said, "Don't worry about what people think now. Think about whether your children and grandchildren will think you have done well."

LORD MOUNTBATTEN

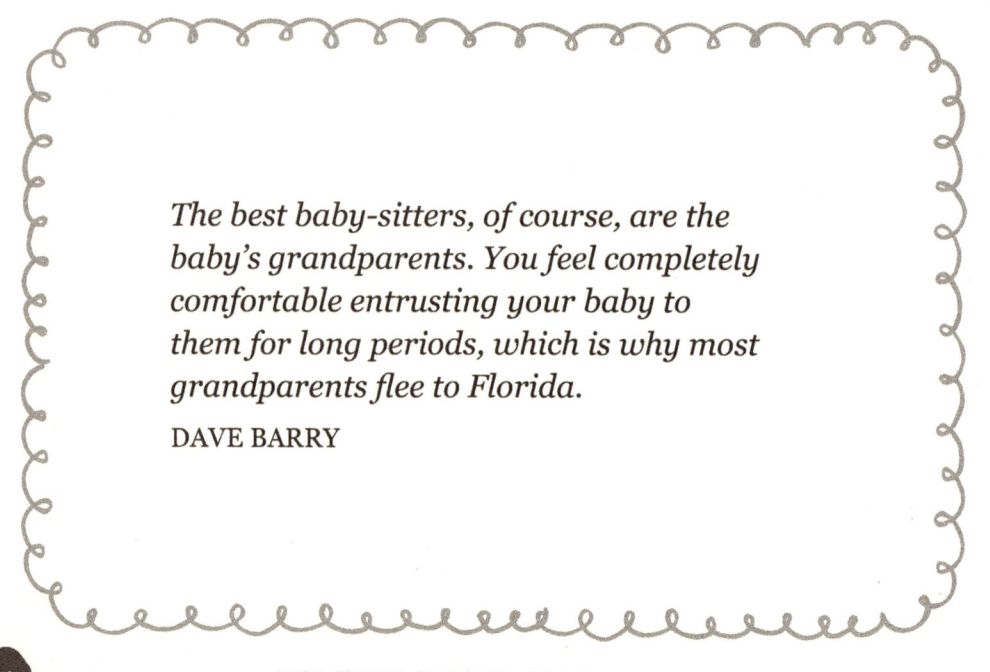

The best baby-sitters, of course, are the baby's grandparents. You feel completely comfortable entrusting your baby to them for long periods, which is why most grandparents flee to Florida.

DAVE BARRY

Before a grandchild is born, grandparents have often come to believe that others don't want to hear those family stories: "Oh, Dad! Not that old one!" "Mum! You've told us about that twice this week already!" But the birth of a grandchild changes everything.

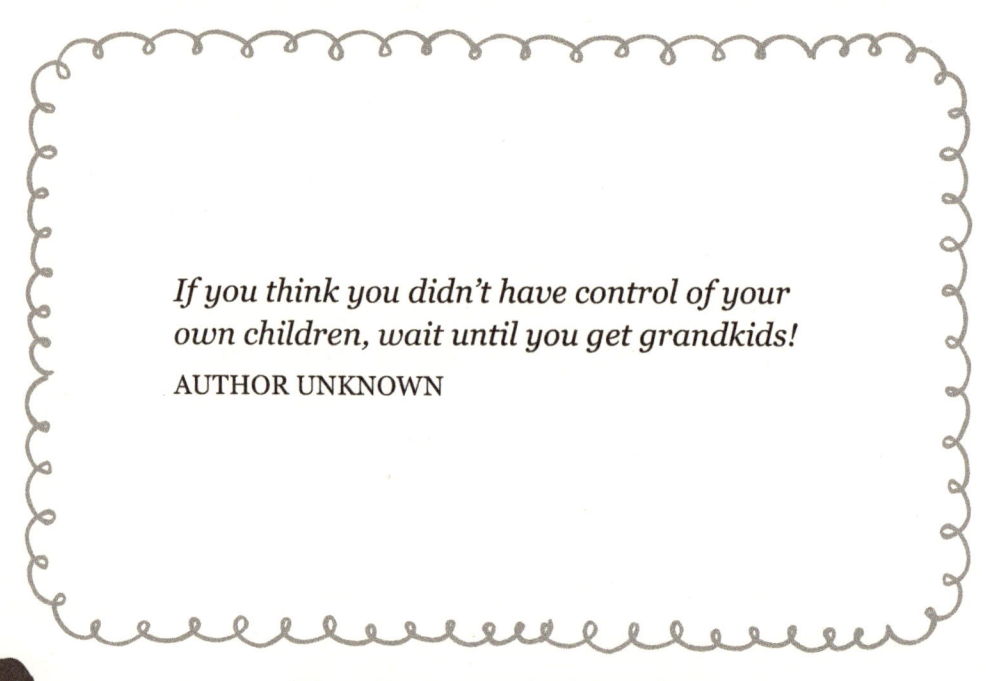

If you think you didn't have control of your own children, wait until you get grandkids!

AUTHOR UNKNOWN

The history of our grandparents is remembered not with rose petals but in the laughter and tears of their children and their children's children. It is into us that the lives of grandparents have gone. It is in us that their history becomes a future.

CHARLES AND ANN MORSE

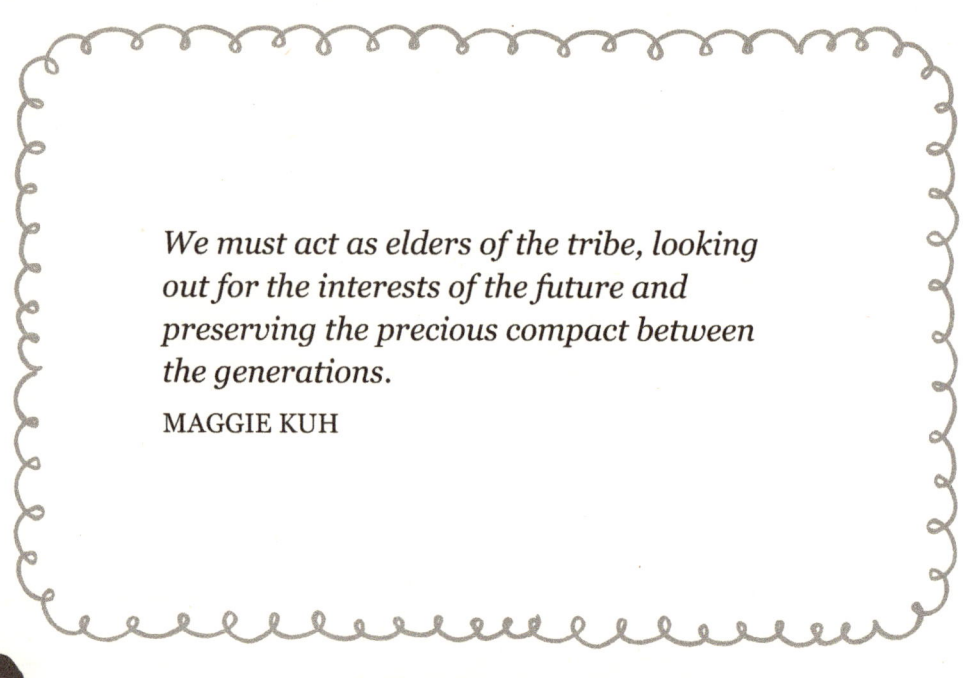

We must act as elders of the tribe, looking out for the interests of the future and preserving the precious compact between the generations.

MAGGIE KUH

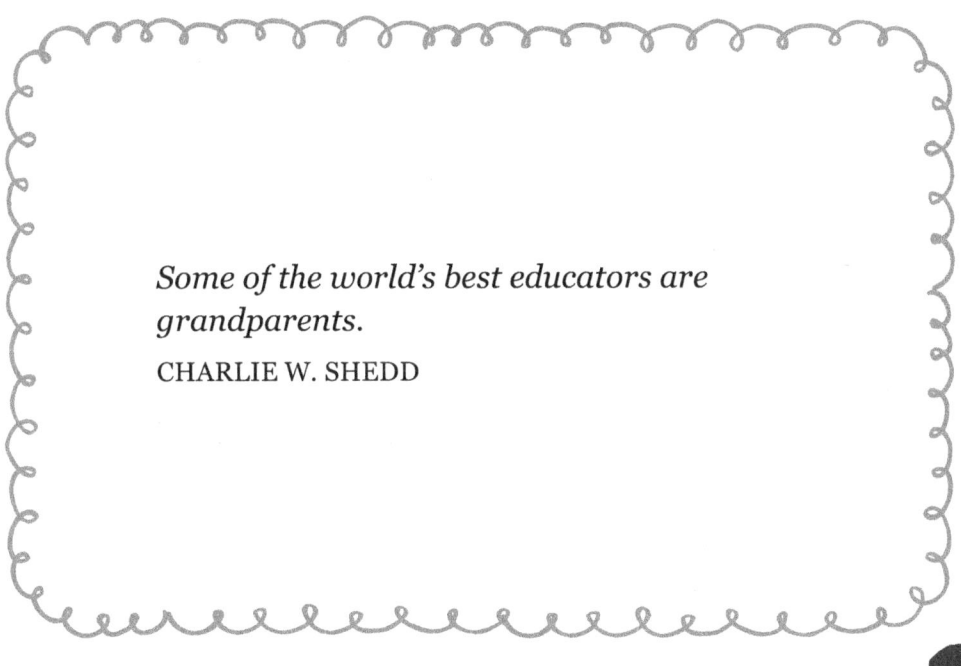

Some of the world's best educators are grandparents.

CHARLIE W. SHEDD

Who knows what goes on in the mind of a child that makes them really yearn to visit their grandparents? I once asked my son why he liked visiting my mother so much. He answered in a heartbeat, "Nanny Mabel does me fried eggs." I remember thinking, "Fried eggs? I'm slogging to earn the money to buy you computers, bicycles and holidays, and Nanny Mabel gets an accolade for fried eggs!"

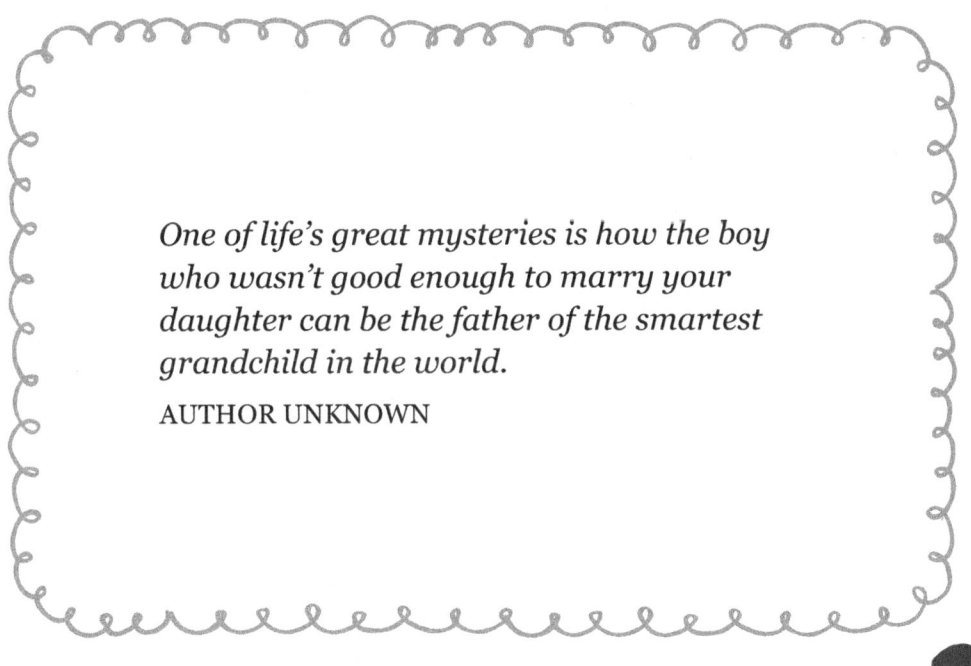

One of life's great mysteries is how the boy who wasn't good enough to marry your daughter can be the father of the smartest grandchild in the world.

AUTHOR UNKNOWN

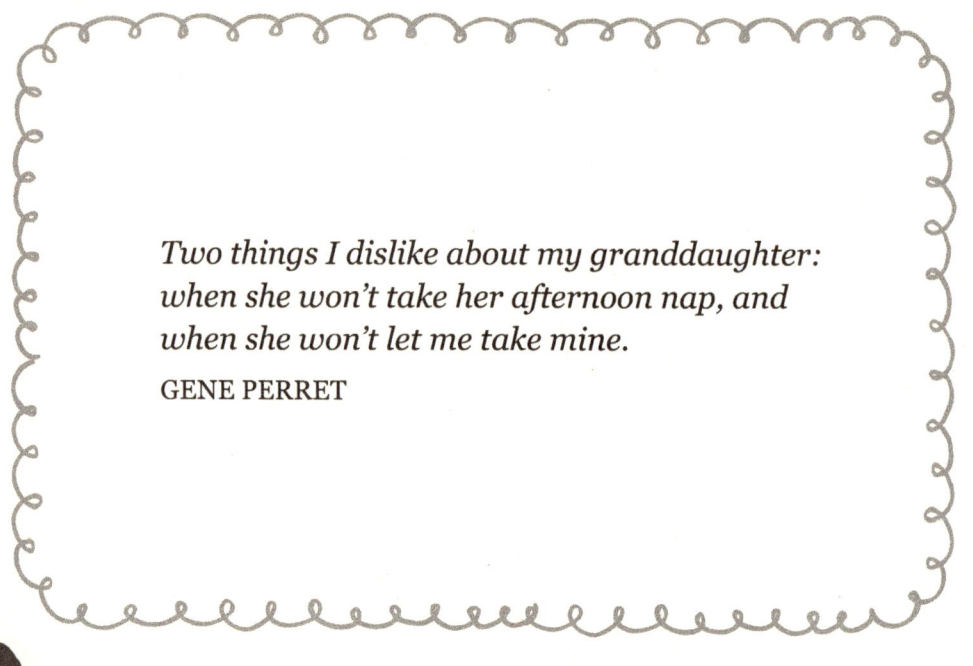

Two things I dislike about my granddaughter: when she won't take her afternoon nap, and when she won't let me take mine.

GENE PERRET

Share the past with your grandchildren. Take them to see your old home or tell them about anything at all that was significant to you: your first school, your first job, the first time you kissed their grandfather. Don't let the cynicism of the world rob you or your grandchildren of these moments. Have the courage to grasp hold of them for yourself – and to pass them on.

I miss him still today: his long, whiskery eyebrows, his huge hands and hugs, his warmth, his prayers, his stories, but above all his shining example of how to live and how to die.

BEAR GRYLLS

Grandchildren don't make a woman feel old; it's being married to a grandfather that bothers her.

AUTHOR UNKNOWN

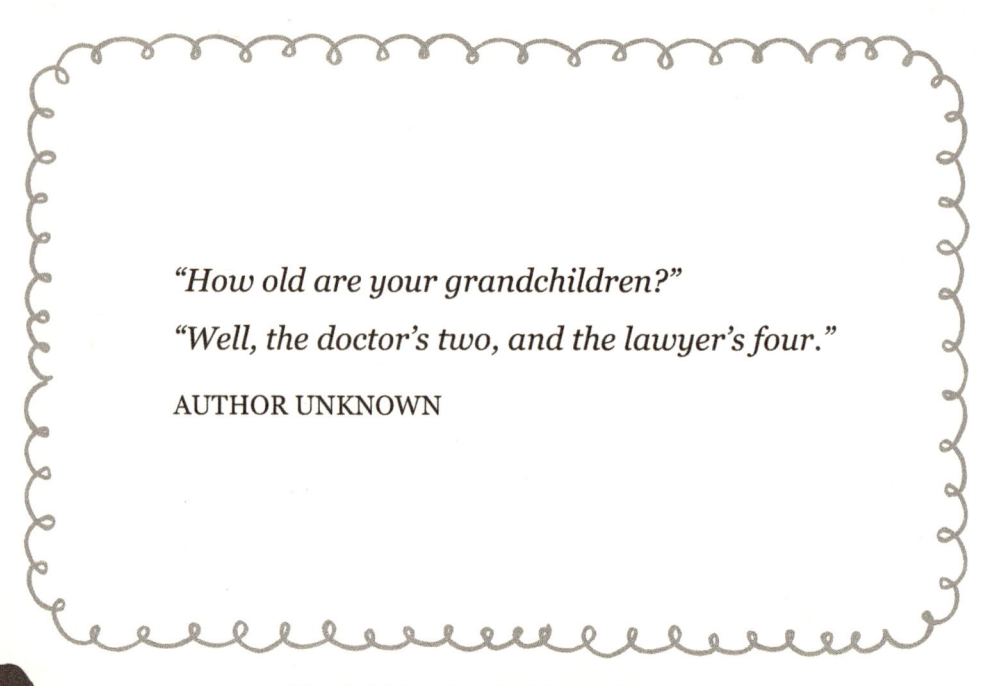

"How old are your grandchildren?"

"Well, the doctor's two, and the lawyer's four."

AUTHOR UNKNOWN

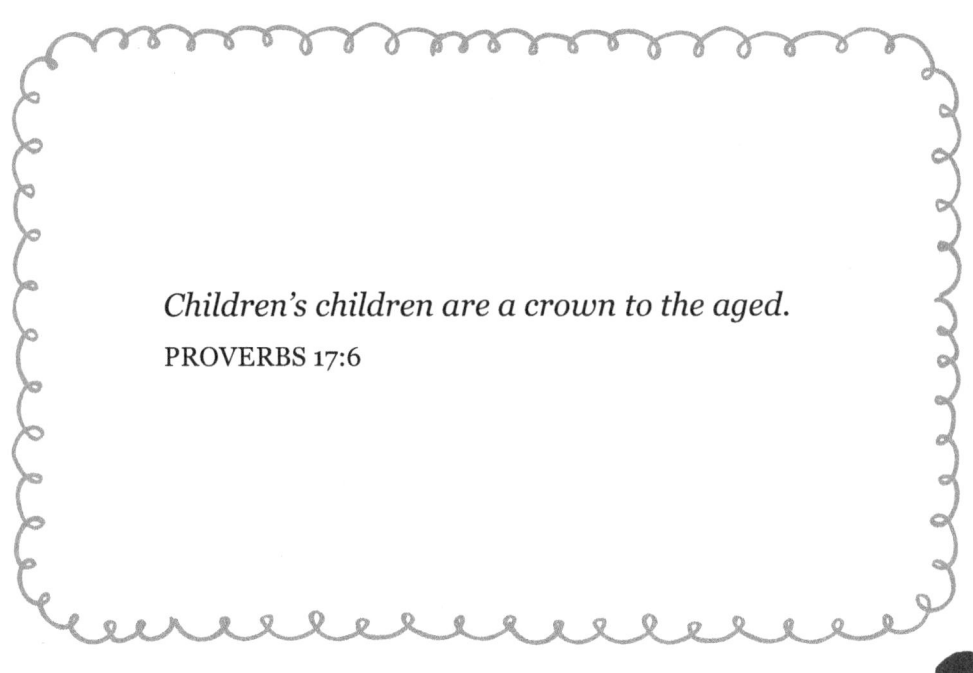

Children's children are a crown to the aged.
PROVERBS 17:6

Grandparents' answerphone

Hello. Please listen to the following options:

- *If you are one of our four children, press 1 and then press from 1 to 4 according to the order of your birth so we know who it is.*
- *If you need us to stay with the grandchildren, press 2.*
- *If you want to borrow the car, press 3.*
- *If you want us to do your washing and ironing, press 4.*

- *If you want the grandchildren to sleep here tonight, press 5.*
- *If you want us to pick up the kids from school, press 6.*
- *If you want us to shop for and/or prepare a meal press 7.*
- *If you want to come to eat here on Sunday, press 8.*
- *If you need money, press 9.*

If you are going to invite us to dinner or take us to a restaurant, start talking now – we are listening!

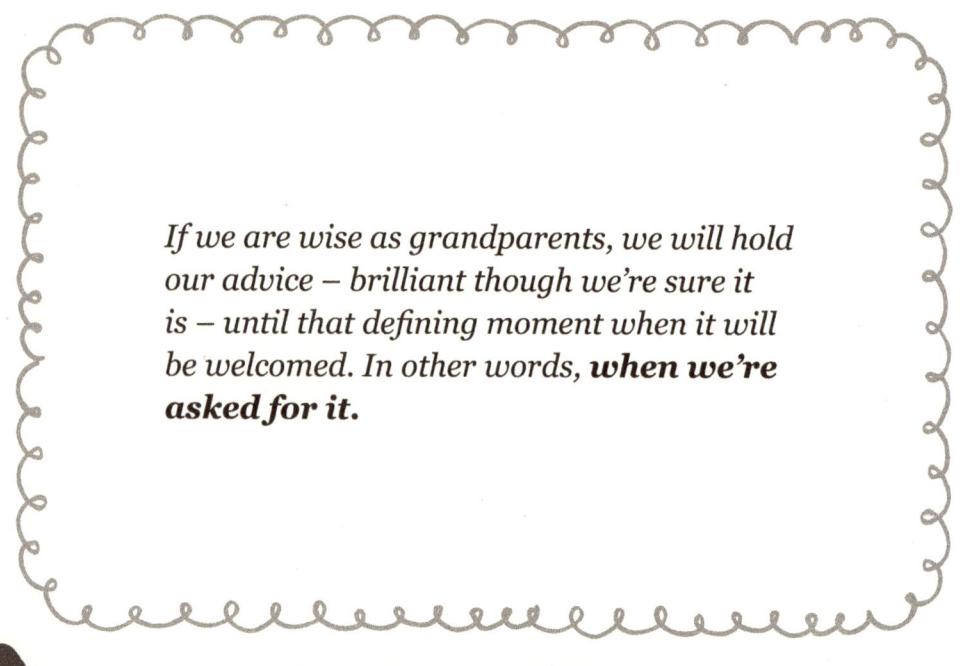

If we are wise as grandparents, we will hold our advice – brilliant though we're sure it is – until that defining moment when it will be welcomed. In other words, **when we're asked for it.**

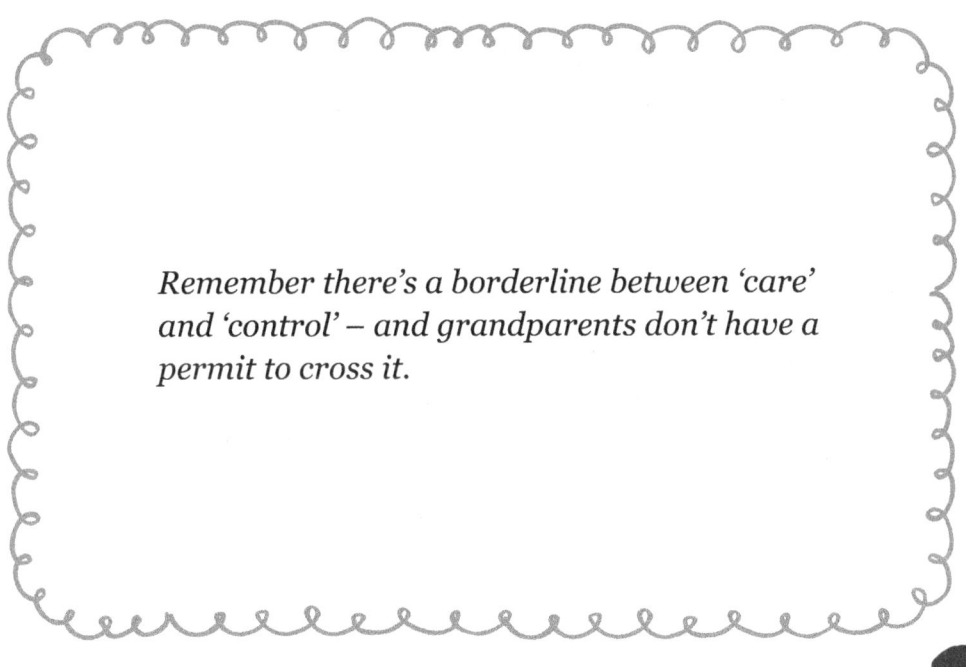

Remember there's a borderline between 'care' and 'control' – and grandparents don't have a permit to cross it.

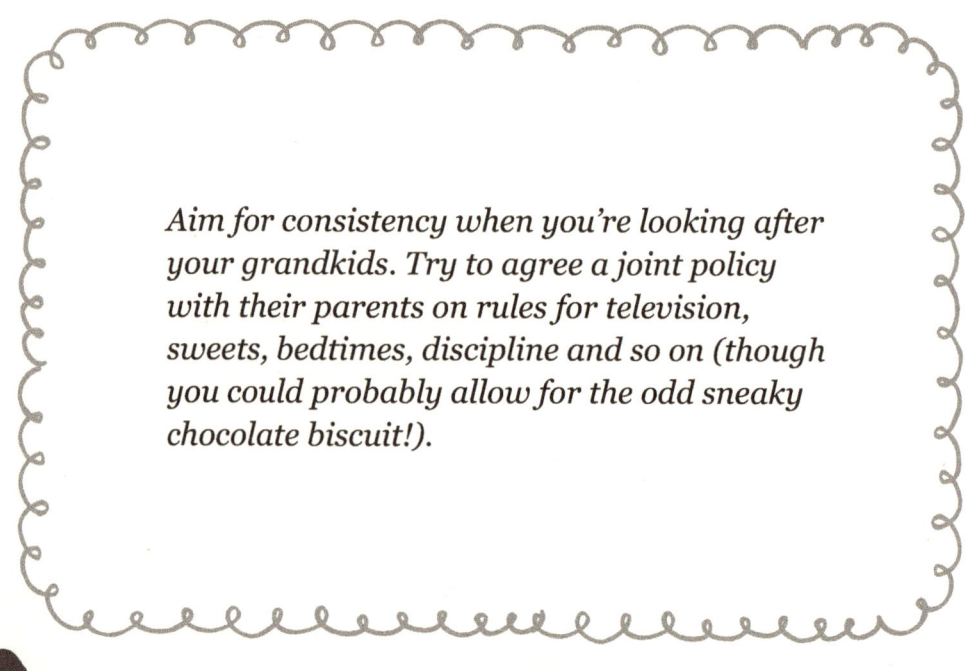

Aim for consistency when you're looking after your grandkids. Try to agree a joint policy with their parents on rules for television, sweets, bedtimes, discipline and so on (though you could probably allow for the odd sneaky chocolate biscuit!).

Becoming a grandmother is wonderful. One moment you're just a mother. The next you are all-wise and prehistoric.

PAM BROWN

Grandfathers do have a special place in the lives of their children's children. They can delight and play with them and even indulge them in ways that they did not indulge their own children. Grandfather knows that after the fun and games are over with his adorable grandchildren he can return to the quiet of his own home and peacefully reflect on this phenomenon of fatherhood.

ALVIN F. POUSSAINT

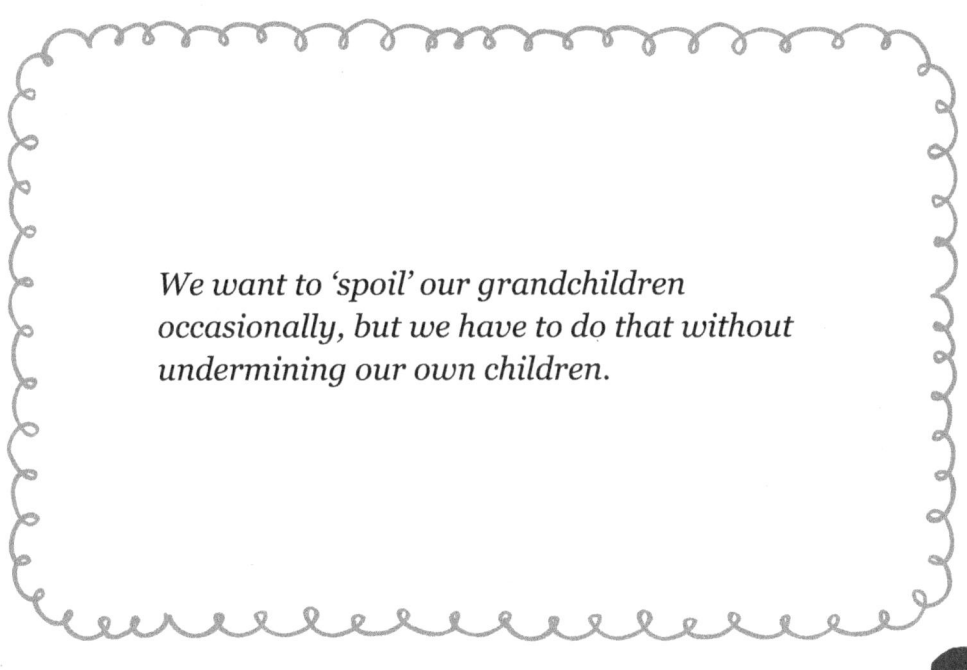

We want to 'spoil' our grandchildren occasionally, but we have to do that without undermining our own children.

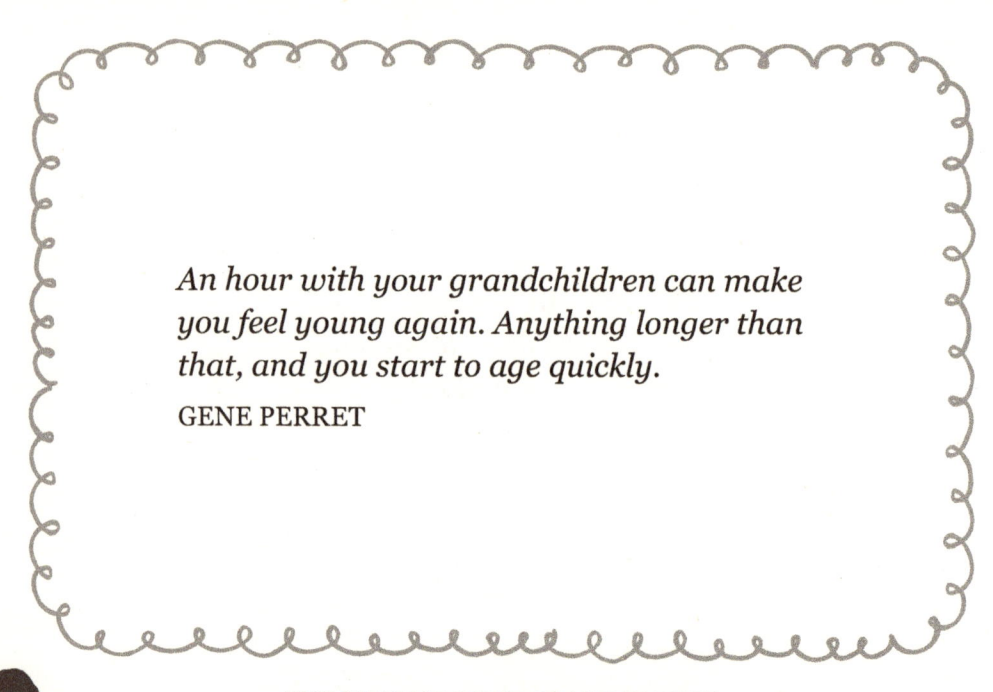

An hour with your grandchildren can make you feel young again. Anything longer than that, and you start to age quickly.

GENE PERRET

The grandchildren were always delighted to see her. Why? They enjoyed her because she obviously enjoyed them.

PEREGRINE CHURCHILL,
GRANDSON OF LADY RANDOLPH CHURCHILL

Create scrapbooks of your visits with your grandchildren – photographs, tickets, brochures, stories. Make sure you capture those memories to share later.

THE SIXTY SECOND GRANDPARENT

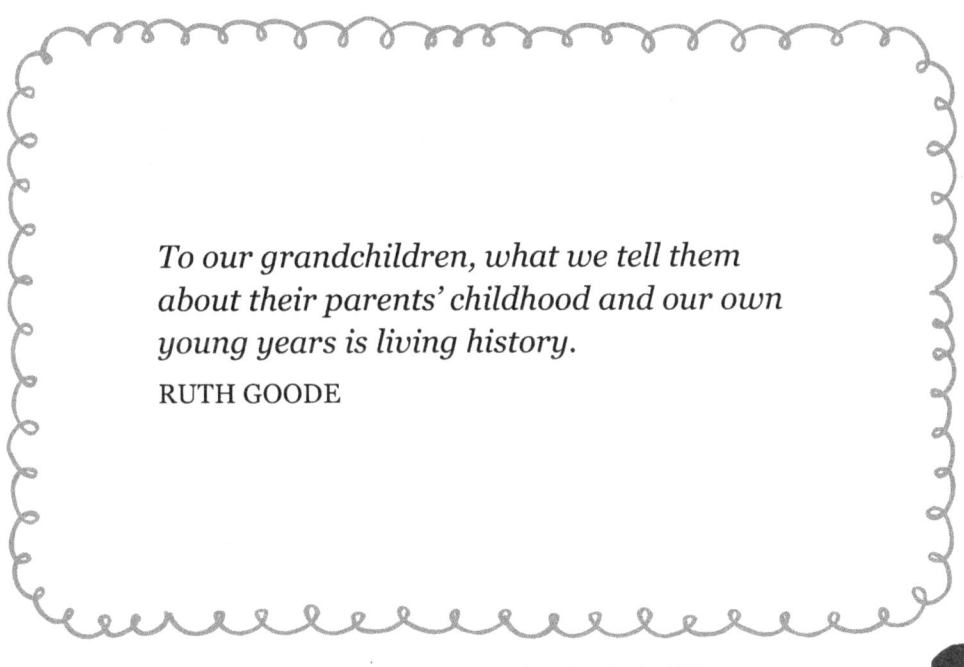

To our grandchildren, what we tell them about their parents' childhood and our own young years is living history.

RUTH GOODE

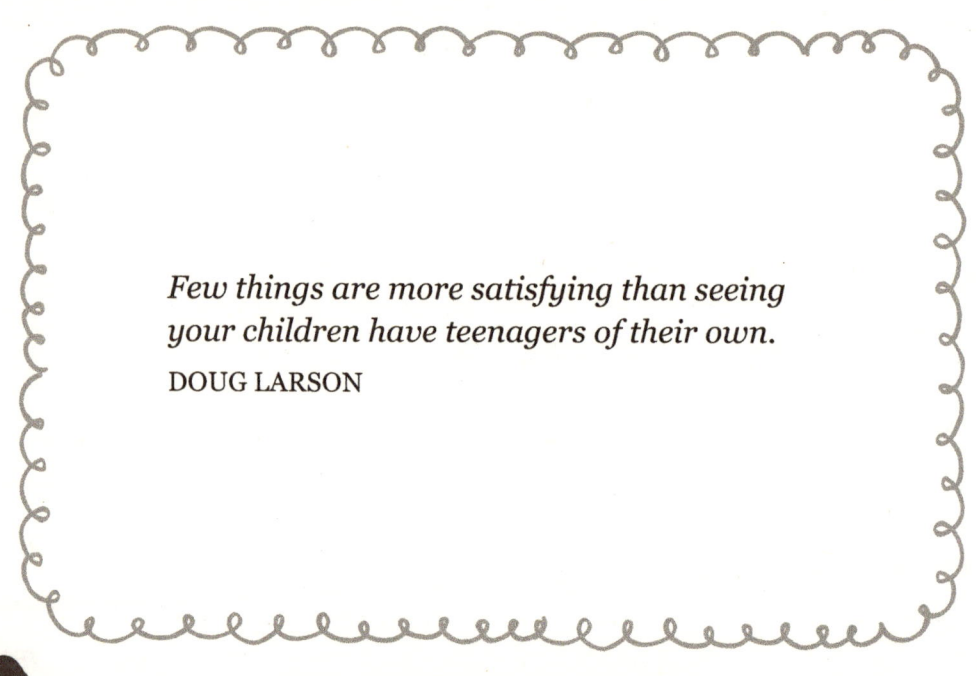

Few things are more satisfying than seeing your children have teenagers of their own.

DOUG LARSON

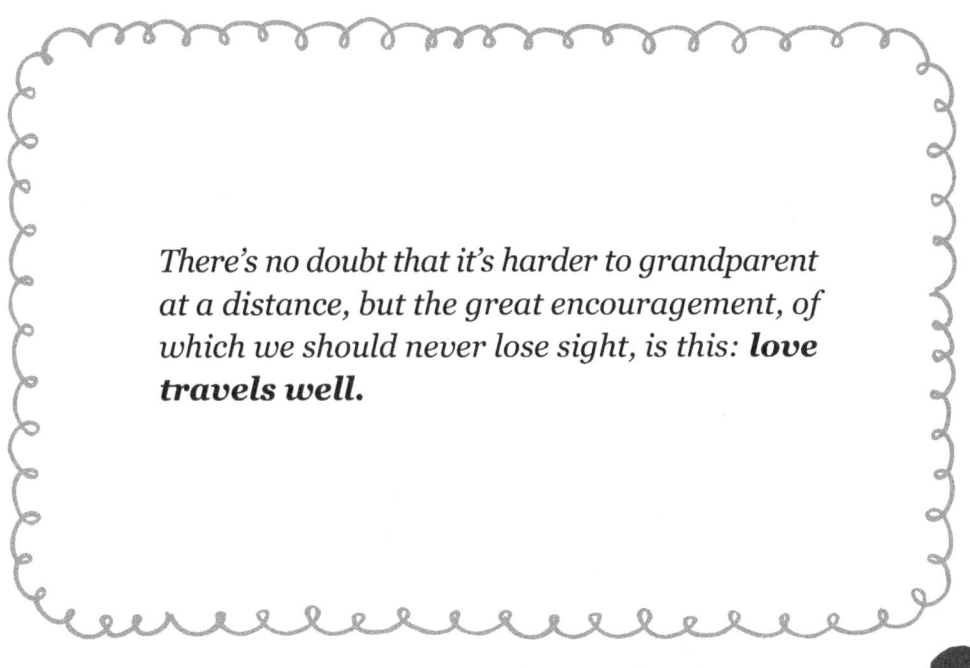

*There's no doubt that it's harder to grandparent at a distance, but the great encouragement, of which we should never lose sight, is this: **love travels well.***

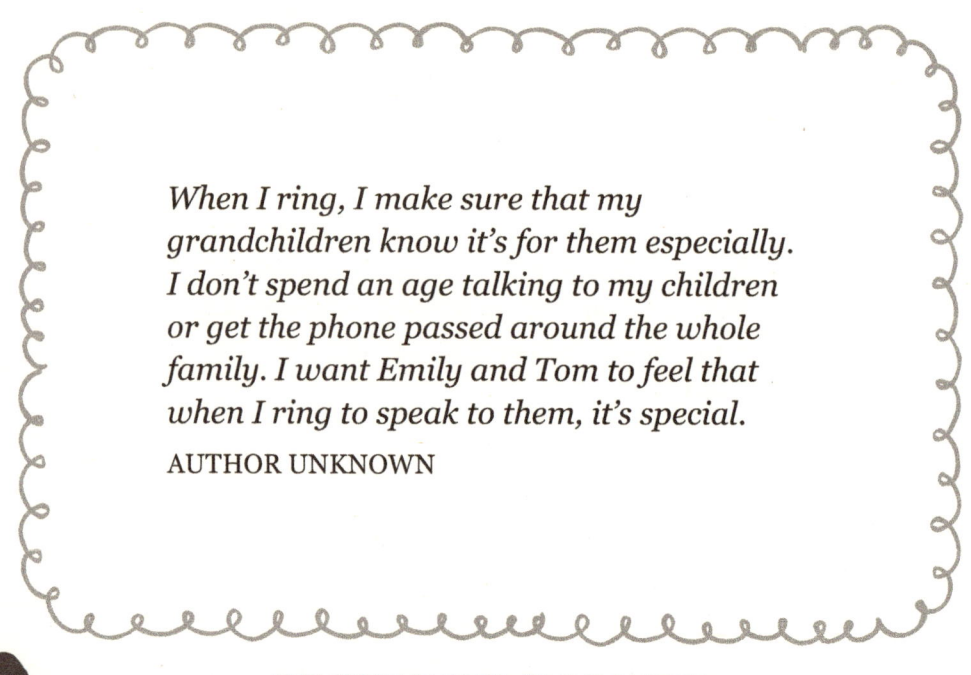

When I ring, I make sure that my grandchildren know it's for them especially. I don't spend an age talking to my children or get the phone passed around the whole family. I want Emily and Tom to feel that when I ring to speak to them, it's special.

AUTHOR UNKNOWN

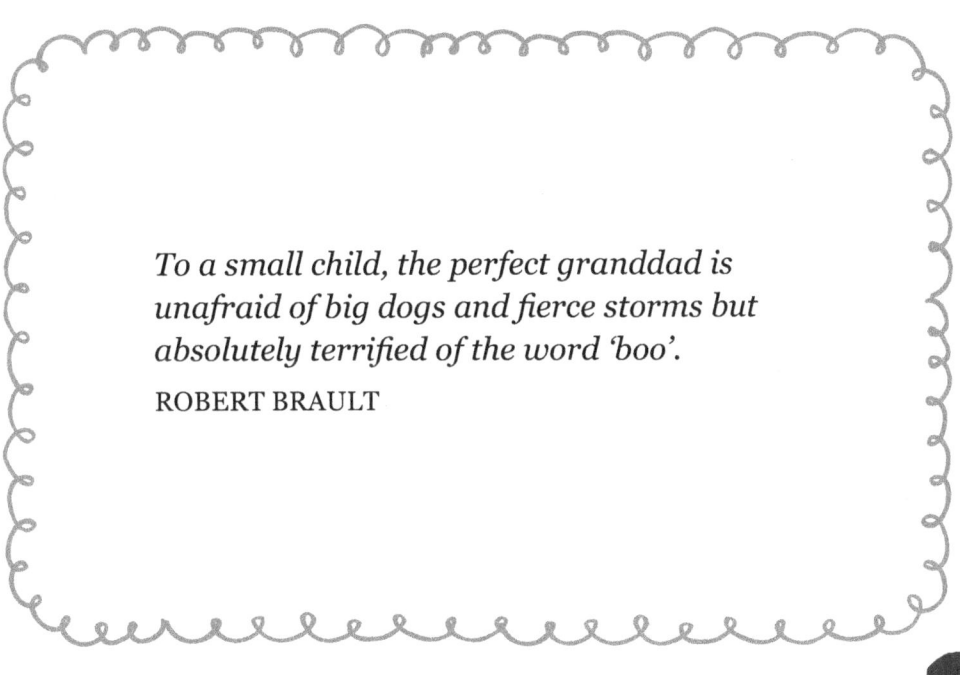

To a small child, the perfect granddad is unafraid of big dogs and fierce storms but absolutely terrified of the word 'boo'.

ROBERT BRAULT

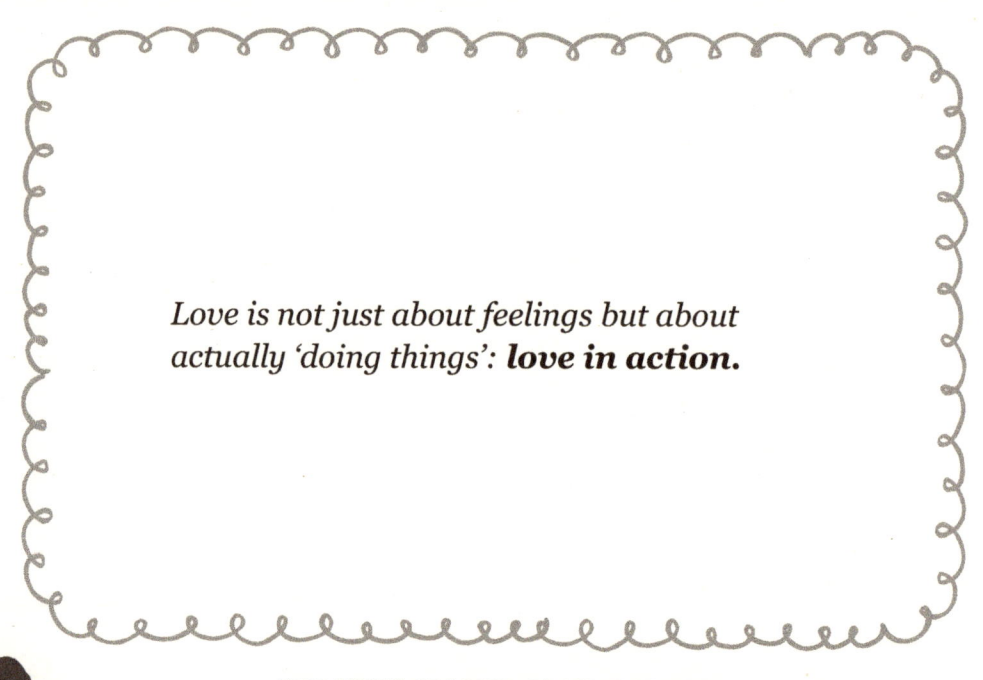

Love is not just about feelings but about actually 'doing things': **love in action.**

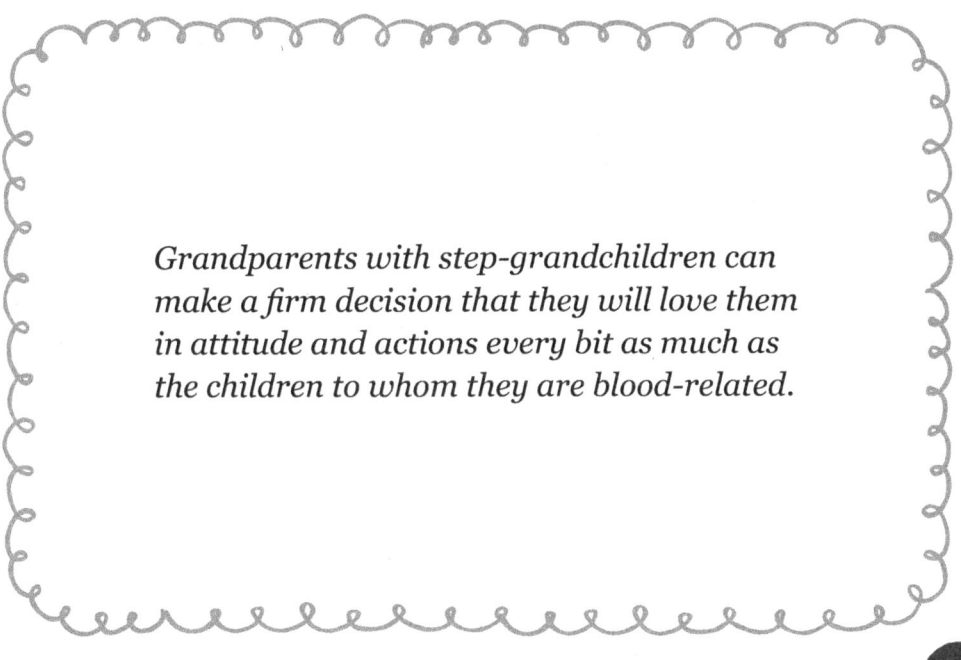

Grandparents with step-grandchildren can make a firm decision that they will love them in attitude and actions every bit as much as the children to whom they are blood-related.

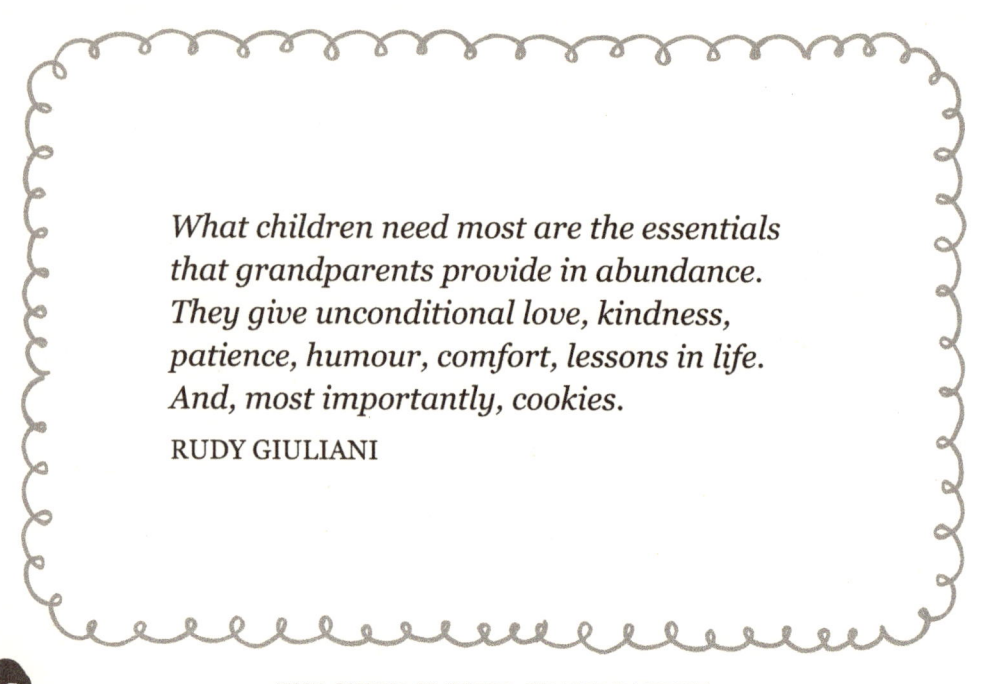

What children need most are the essentials that grandparents provide in abundance. They give unconditional love, kindness, patience, humour, comfort, lessons in life. And, most importantly, cookies.

RUDY GIULIANI

When we grandparent from a distance we can face many difficulties, but the rewards can be great. One child put it like this: "My grandmother really loves me. Even though I live hundreds of miles away from her, I talk to her almost every day. Sometimes she sends me stamps for my collection and she sends me jokes on my mobile. I think when I'm older I would like to live near my gran."

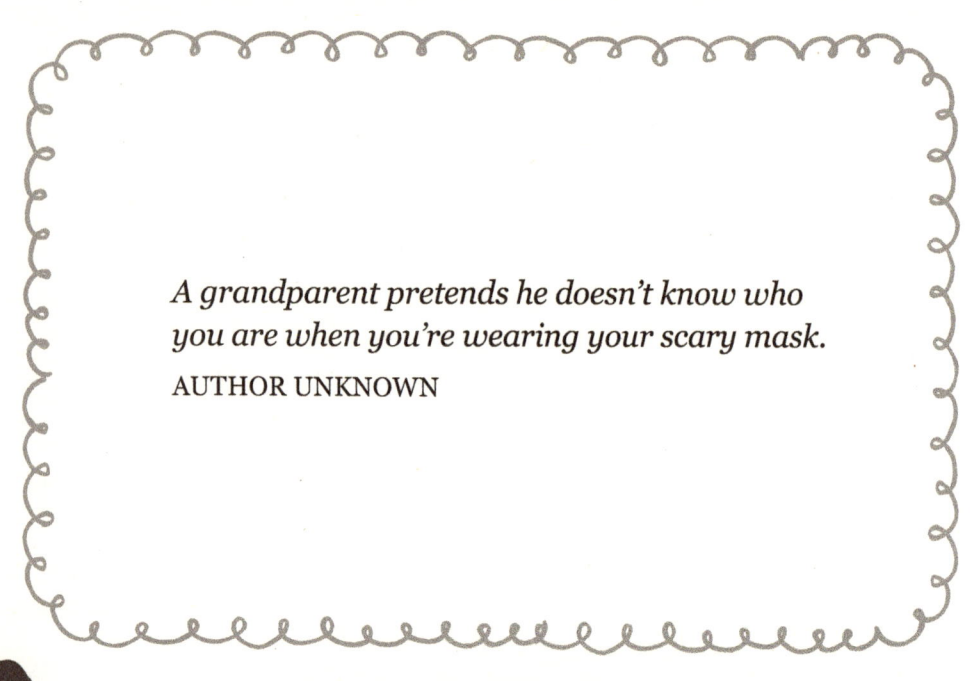

A grandparent pretends he doesn't know who you are when you're wearing your scary mask.

AUTHOR UNKNOWN

When my grandson asked me how old I was, I teasingly replied, "I'm not sure."

"Look in your underwear, Grandpa," he advised. "Mine says I'm four to six."

AUTHOR UNKNOWN

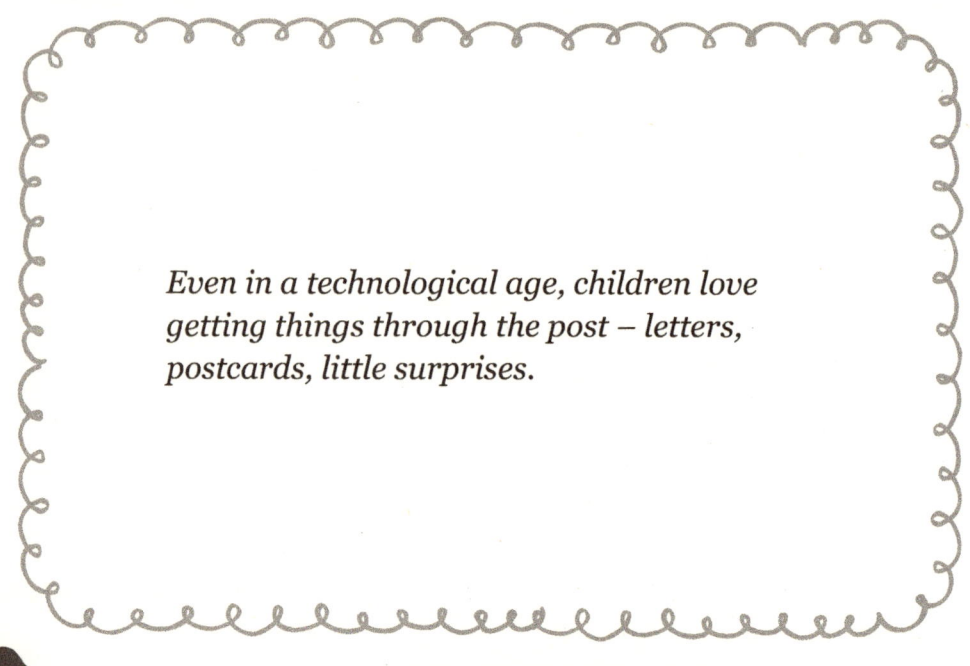

Even in a technological age, children love getting things through the post – letters, postcards, little surprises.

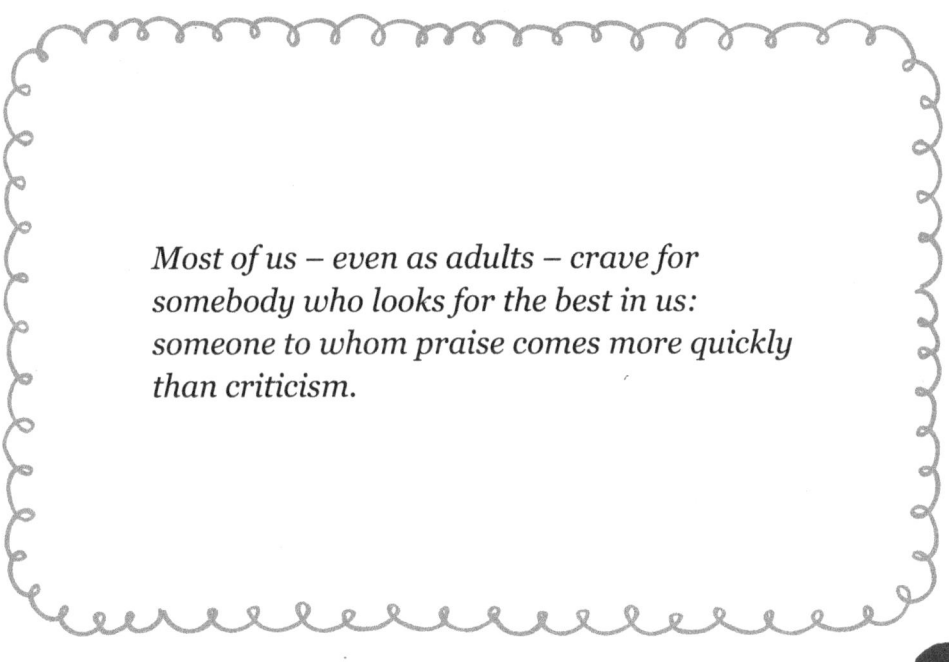

Most of us – even as adults – crave for somebody who looks for the best in us: someone to whom praise comes more quickly than criticism.

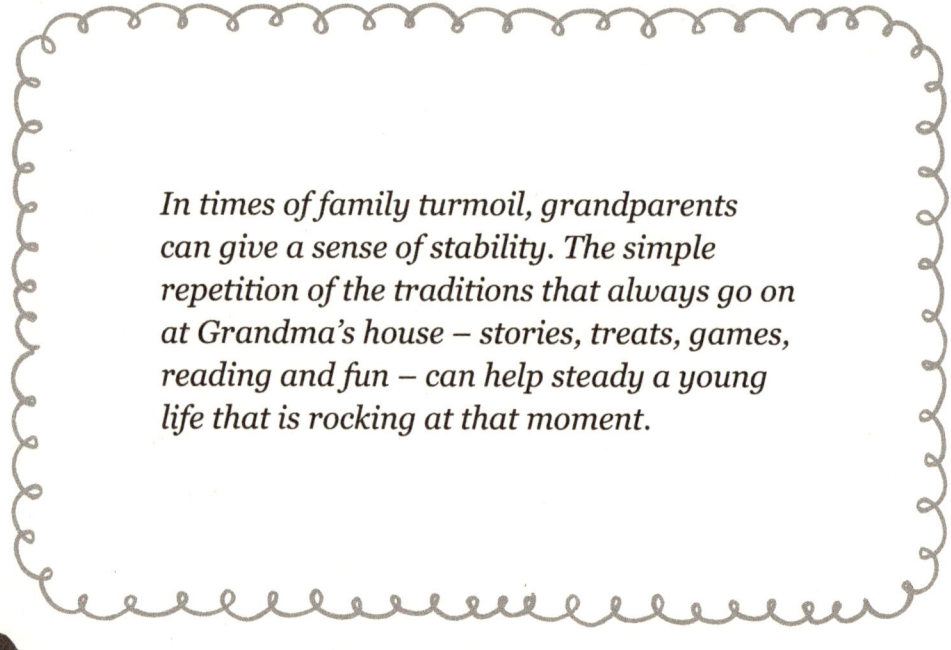

In times of family turmoil, grandparents can give a sense of stability. The simple repetition of the traditions that always go on at Grandma's house – stories, treats, games, reading and fun – can help steady a young life that is rocking at that moment.

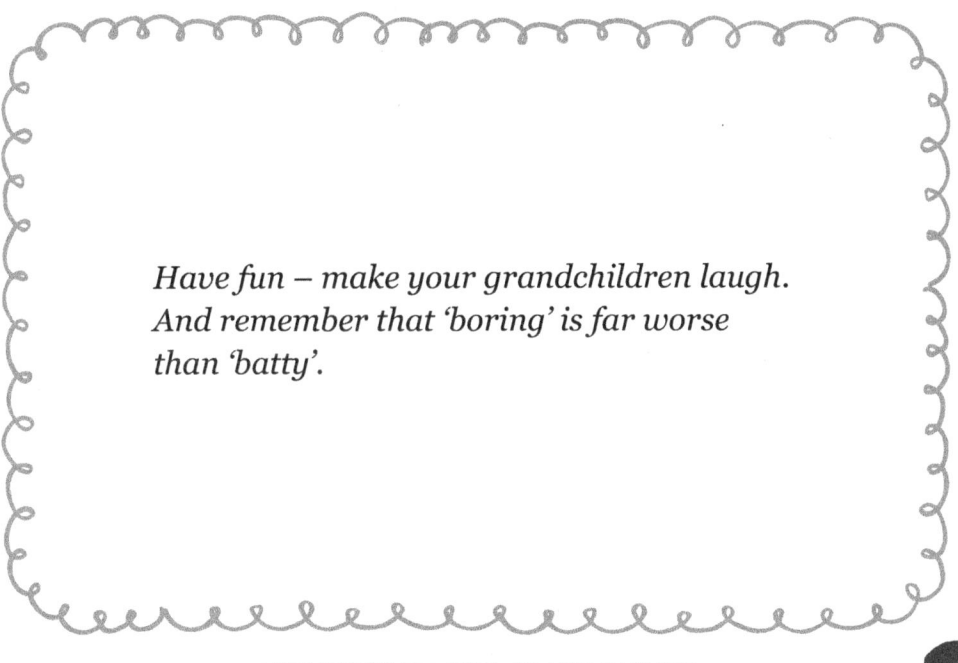

Have fun – make your grandchildren laugh. And remember that 'boring' is far worse than 'batty'.

I have a warm feeling after playing with my grandchildren. It's the liniment working.

AUTHOR UNKNOWN

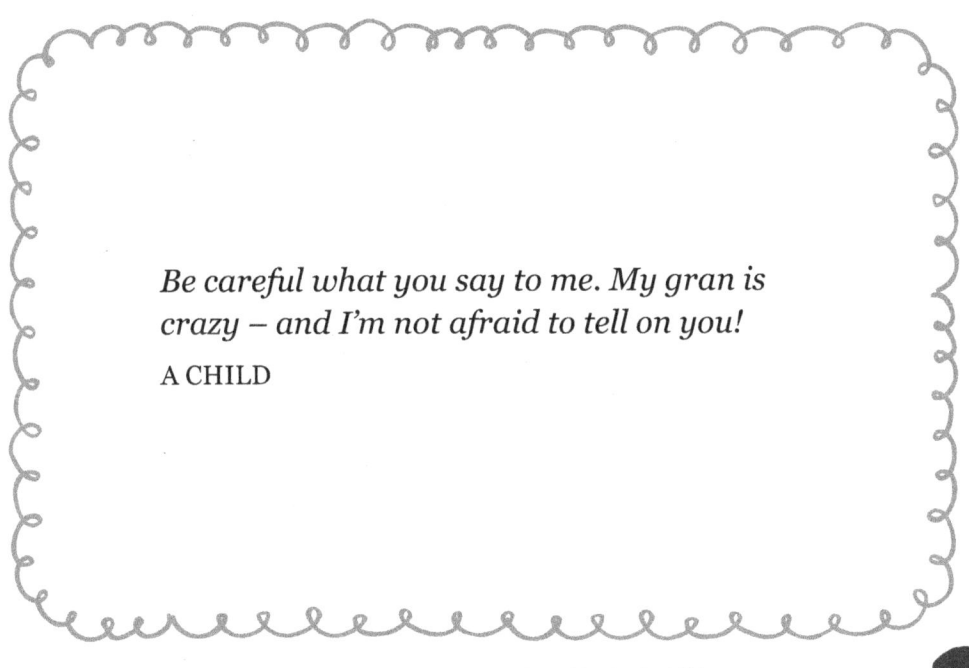

Be careful what you say to me. My gran is crazy – and I'm not afraid to tell on you!

A CHILD

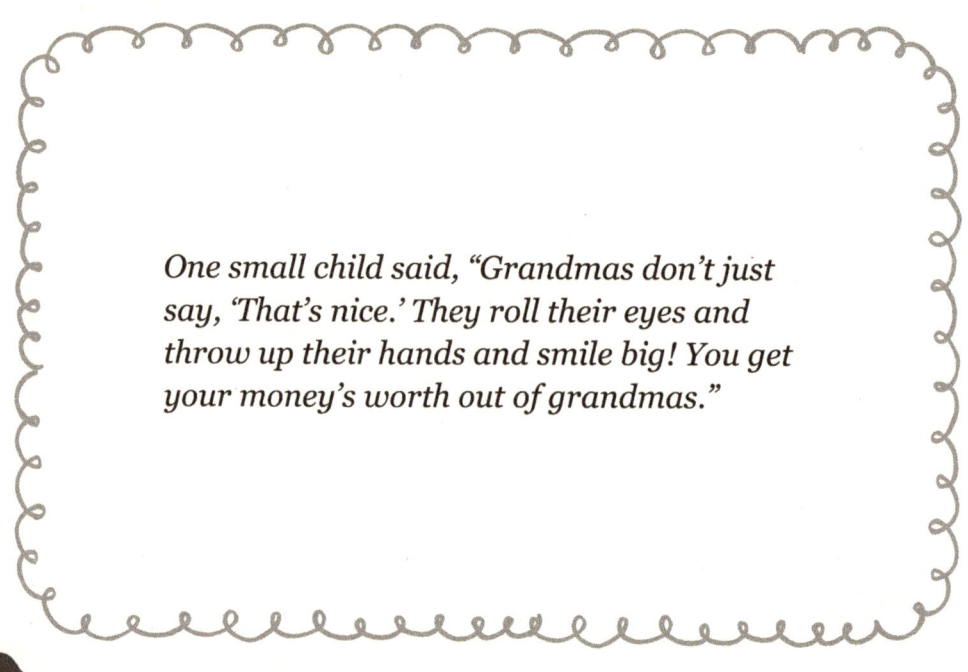

One small child said, "Grandmas don't just say, 'That's nice.' They roll their eyes and throw up their hands and smile big! You get your money's worth out of grandmas."

Imagine having somebody who, when you are grown and perhaps have been written off by almost everybody else, took time to write to you, to ring you – even, perhaps, to pray for you.

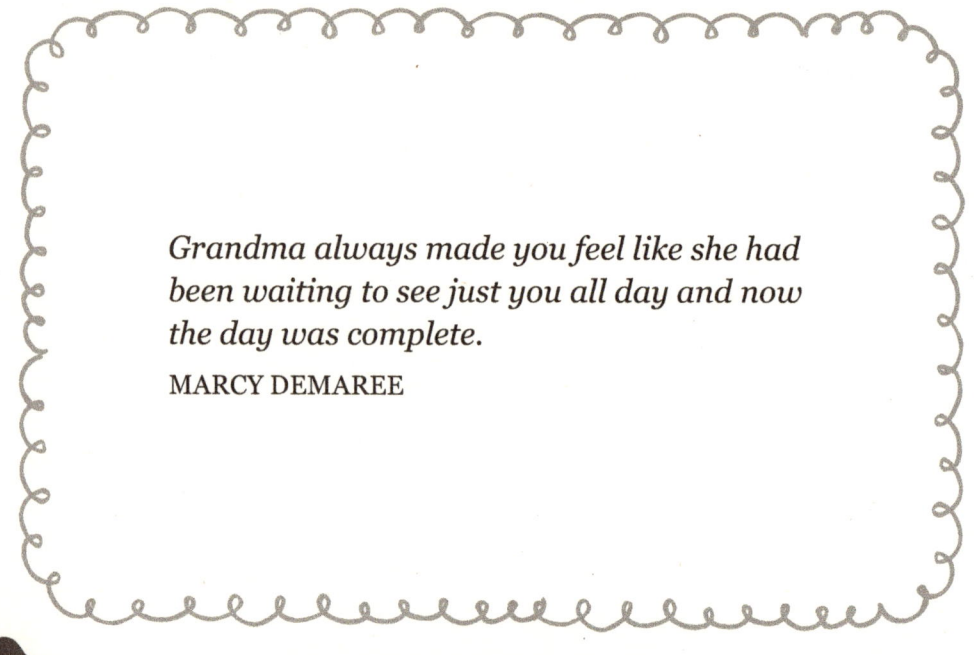

Grandma always made you feel like she had been waiting to see just you all day and now the day was complete.

MARCY DEMAREE

Grandchildren have taught me how important the future is. I try to look through their eyes and envision what's in their imagination. What's the world going to look like when they're my age? That really does take a huge imagination.

RICHARD LUGAR

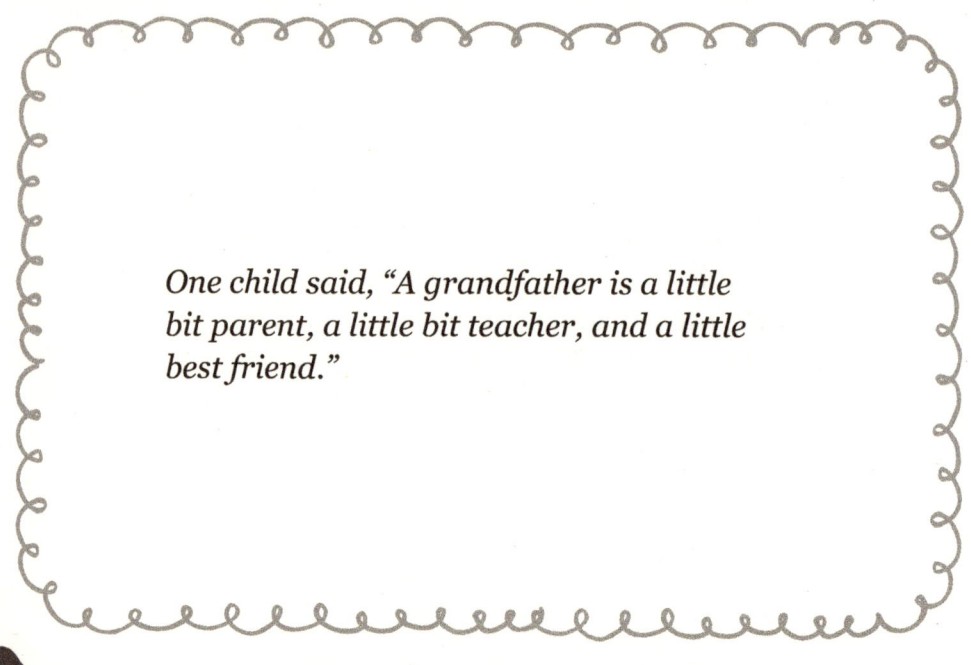

One child said, "A grandfather is a little bit parent, a little bit teacher, and a little best friend."

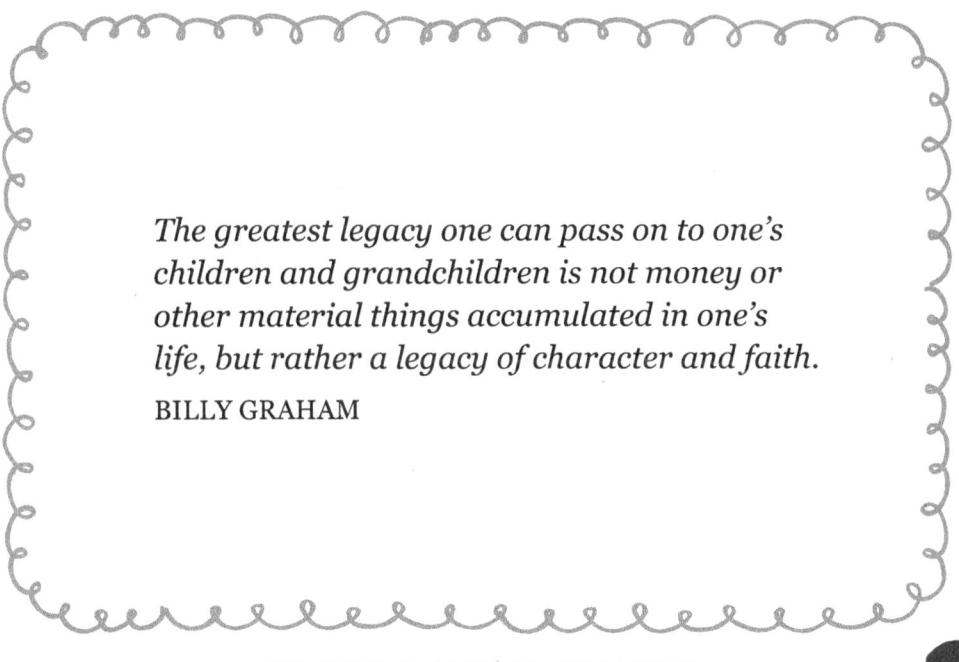

The greatest legacy one can pass on to one's children and grandchildren is not money or other material things accumulated in one's life, but rather a legacy of character and faith.

BILLY GRAHAM

For many grandparents there is a reward that we will keep as a secret from our children. To them we are responsible older people who lavish love and care on their darling offspring because we are such wonderful, selfless people. But what we hope they never realise is that for some of us the reason is much simpler ...

... Grandparents get to play again.

About Care for the Family

Care for the Family is a registered charity and has been working to strengthen family life since 1988. Our aim is to promote strong family relationships and to help those who face family difficulties. Working throughout the UK and the Isle of Man, we provide parenting, relationship and bereavement support through our events, courses, training, volunteer networks and a great range of DVDs, books and online resources.

Our work is motivated by Christian compassion, and our resources and support are available to everyone, of any faith or none.

To find out more, visit www.careforthefamily.org.uk